MAY YOU ENJOY THIS BOOK

The Public Library is free to everyone living in
Nashua. You can increase its usefulness to all by
returning books promptly, on or before the "Date
Due" as stamped.

If you derive pleasure and profit from the use of
your Public Library, why not tell others about its
many services.

THE NASHUA PUBLIC LIBRARY
Nashua, N.H.

GAYLORD MG

Remapping Southern Literature

Remapping Southern Literature

CONTEMPORARY SOUTHERN WRITERS

AND THE WEST

Robert H. Brinkmeyer Jr.

MERCER UNIVERSITY

LAMAR MEMORIAL LECTURES NO. 42

The University of Georgia Press
Athens and London

810. 9975
B
B98'
NPL

© 2000 by the University of Georgia Press

Athens, Georgia 30602

All rights reserved

Designed by Betty P. McDaniel

Set in 10/15 Electra by G&S Typesetters, Inc.

Printed and bound by Maple-Vail Book Manufacturing Group

The paper in this book meets the guidelines for

permanence and durability of the Committee on

Production Guidelines for Book Longevity of the

Council on Library Resources.

Printed in the United States of America

04   03   02   01   00   C   5   4   3   2   1

Library of Congress Cataloging-in-Publication Data

Brinkmeyer, Robert H.

   Remapping southern literature: contemporary Southern writers
and the West / Robert H. Brinkmeyer, Jr.

      p. cm. — (Mercer University Lamar memorial lectures ;
   no. 42)

Includes bibliographical references and index.

ISBN 0-8203-2189-3 (alk. paper)

   1. American literature — Southern States — History and
criticism.   2. American literature — West (U.S.) — History and
criticism.   3. Southern States — In literature.   4. West (U.S.) —
In literature.   5. Regionalism in literature.   I. Title.   II. Series.

PS261 .B745 2000

810.9'975 21— dc21

                                                            99-043731

British Library Cataloging-in-Publication Data available

for Peter Brown,

who exemplifies "regeneration through community"

For the artist to be unwilling to move, mentally or spiritually or physically, out of the familiar is a sign that spiritual timidity or poverty or decay has come upon him; for what is familiar will then have turned into all that is tyrannical.

EUDORA WELTY, "Place in Fiction"

Contents

Abbreviations

Foreword

When the Lamar Lectures Committee meets to choose the scholars it will nominate as lecturers to Mercer University's president, it tries to select those writers whose abilities are most likely to enable it to fulfill the terms of Eugenia Dorothy Blount Lamar's bequest: to present lectures of "the very highest type of scholarship" that will "aid in the permanent preservation of the values of southern culture, history, and literature." These criteria are demanding; as a result, most of the forty-two Lamar Lecturers have been prominent senior scholars.

Several times, however, Mercer has been fortunate to invite a younger-but-maturing scholar as he or she was coming into his or her interpretive heights. That happened in 1998. Robert Brinkmeyer was an excellent lecturer, in well-honed language making superb use of his texts, and the audience's responses to his lectures were remarkably lively.

His thesis may be an important new way of thinking about Southern literature. Instead of the north-south axis on which both Southern popular culture and Southern renaissance literature have rotated, Professor Brinkmeyer proposes that we may learn still more by imagining an east-west axis, with the East standing for such values as place, rootedness, home, and community and the West standing for values like space, freedom, pioneering, and individualism. After showing how Southern renaissance literature symbolically represents the South as the East, Professor Brinkmeyer's lectures led us into a symbolic West that began long ago with James Fenimore Cooper but began in Southern literature with James Dickey's *Deliverance* and has now become a literal as well as figurative place in the work of Cormac McCarthy and others. In his third lecture Professor Brinkmeyer argued that there is a stance in very recent novels in which Southern writers look back at the South from the West.

An added pleasure for the hosts of the 1998 Lamar Lectures was the presence of Debra Rae Cohen, Professor Brinkmeyer's wife and also a literary scholar, and several University of Mississippi graduate students, who made the long drive from Oxford to Macon to hear their teacher.

Robert Brinkmeyer shows us how boundaries of value and meaning are being explored, crossed, broken, and recrossed in contemporary Southern literature. Mrs. Lamar, thinking about the future in 1955, could not have foreseen that "permanent preservation" would involve the chronicling and interpretation of so much change — and yet, as the closing pages of these Lectures suggest, the South endures.

> *Michael M. Cass*
> for the Lamar Memorial Lectures Committee

Preface

I first became aware of the Lamar Lectures years ago as a graduate student at the University of North Carolina. I remember sitting in Louis Rubin's office and seeing on his bookshelf a matched set of bound Lamar Lectures, including his own contribution, *The Writer in the South*. After a bit of investigating in the library, I realized how rich the Lamar series was, and since then I have always eagerly awaited the newest addition, looking to the Lamar Lectures as a weathervane of what is new and exciting in the field of Southern studies.

At some point in my career, on those days when I was puffing myself up, I began to fantasize about being asked to give the Lamar Lectures. Such thoughts, though, were the stuff of dreams and desire, not of the here-and-now. Yet fantasy suddenly materialized into reality when out of the blue I received a letter in 1994 from Michael Cass inviting me to the deliver the 1998 Lectures. I will not go into any detail about my feelings upon reading the letter, except to say I felt good. Real good.

Feeling good has pretty much been my entire experience throughout the process of putting together these lectures, other than a few days when the writing sputtered and stalled. Thinking about Southern literature in the context of the West and Western literature has been a rejuvenating intellectual jolt, forcing me not only to extend my reading into the literature of another region — a very happy endeavor — but also, even more significantly, to reconfigure my thoughts on the context of Southern literature and the significance of regionalism and regional identity in modern and postmodern America.

Happy also was my visit to Macon and Mercer University to deliver the lectures. My wife and I were overwhelmed with hospitality and grace, most particularly from Michael and Lynn Cass, our primary hosts, who led us to share in their enthusiasm for Macon and Mercer. Others deserving thanks include Mercer University's president, R. Kirby Godsey; members of the family of the late Eugenia Dorothy Blount Lamar, whose generous contribution established the Lamar Lecture series; and all the members of the Lamar Committee, not only for inviting me but also for making us feel so welcome and at home and for offering encouragement and feedback during my visit. Peter Brown and Andrew Silver, along with Michael Cass, each delivered a succinct and eloquent introduction to one of the lectures. And the audience for the lectures proved attentive and helpful, asking pertinent questions and giving suggestions.

Others have been helpful along the way as I developed and revised the lectures. Several of my colleagues at the University of Mississippi, including Jay Watson, Charles Wilson, Dan Williams, Ted Ownby, and Charles Eagles, have from the beginning been enormously supportive. Others further afield have contributed their help and advice, particularly Fred Hobson, Richard Gray, and Barbara Bennett. Students in both my undergraduate and graduate seminars at the University of Mississippi helped me hone my ideas and broaden my understanding of contemporary Southern literature. And several graduate students made the trip over to Macon to share in the intellectual and social festivities: Wes Berry, Thomas Easterling, Pete Froehlich, Susan Glisson, John Glass, Kitty Keller, and Jennie Lee added much to the fellowship that quickly developed in Macon over a few brief days.

I also appreciate the institutional support I received from the University of Mississippi while writing the lectures. The Southern Studies Program gave me a course release and the Graduate School's Office of Research and the Department of English awarded me summer grants. Virginia Bollinger, my graduate assistant, helped me tremendously in tracking down material and in proofreading. People at the University of Georgia Press have, as usual and as expected, done a marvelous job shepherding my manuscript through production. Thanks go out to the always gracious Karen Orchard and Kristine Blakeslee at the press and to my copyeditor, Gayle Swanson, professionals one and all.

Closer to home, my daughters, Mary, Eliza, and Emma, have shared in both my enthusiasm and my trepidation — and my joy and honor — in giving the Lamar Lectures. And finally there is my strongest supporter, harshest critic, and most talented editor, Debra Rae Cohen, who is also my wife and partner-in-arms and who deserves more thanks than anyone for helping me throughout the entire project.

Remapping Southern Literature

1 / Embracing Place

In *New Westers: The West in Contemporary American Culture*, Michael L. Johnson explores the recent resurgence of interest in the American West, an interest manifested throughout this country's popular culture from Stetson cologne to the Marlboro man to line dancing to adobe architecture. Although fascination with the West and its towering mythology—a mythology encompassing, to name several things, a rugged individualism, wide-open spaces, and a conquering spirit—has long been a shaping force of the American imagination, Johnson persuasively argues that in the mid–1980s Americans began imaginatively embracing the West with unusual intensity and nostalgia. No doubt the cultural dynamics of this shift are complex and myriad, but Johnson is probably right in suggesting that the recent imaginative lightin' out to the Western frontier is in large part a response to what is perceived as the increasing dehumanization and homogenization of postmodern culture.[1] Out West, the mythology goes, life is as stark and fundamental as the desert land-scape; out in the desert, one can make — or remake — oneself by one's own hand. Out West, too, as Wallace Stegner has noted, lies a "geography of hope," space where a person can leave the past behind and seek the wide-open future, driven by an optimism that configures the West into "a land of Cockaigne, an Indian Valley Line where every day is payday, a Big Rock Candy Mountain where the handouts grow on bushes and the little streams of alcohol come trickling down the rocks."[2] Visions of a free and unencumbered life, even if not as fanciful as Stegner's characterization, no doubt undergird the imaginative needs and desires of those wannabe cowboys and cowgirls whom Johnson designates as the "New Westers."

OK, but what does all this have to do with Southern literature and culture? A lot, actually. Certainly one of most intriguing developments in contemporary Southern fiction is that a number of Southern writers have in a sense become New Westers, imaginatively forsaking Dixie for the West, writing fiction both of the contemporary West, particularly Montana, and of the bygone era of cowboys, Indians, and gunfights — that is, Westerns. Writers from the South who have looked to the West include Doris Betts, Barry Hannah, Cormac McCarthy, Madison Smartt Bell, Richard Ford, Rick Bass, Barbara Kingsolver, Chris Offutt, Frederick Barthelme, and Clyde Edgerton. And just recently, while I was finishing up the lectures on which this book is based, came two more Westering novels, by Southerners Dorothy Allison and Tim Gautreaux.

This striking development raises a number of issues about the very designation "Southern fiction." Should we still call, for instance, Western fiction by Southerners "Southern"? Or should we — as Michael Kowalewski does in his recent book on the literature of the West, identifying four of the Southerners I am talking about in this book as Western writers — call it Western?[3] Or should we look for a new designation suggesting a blurring of regional boundaries, following the lead of the economists who talk of the South and the West as the Sunbelt? Or should we, in these days of the global village and cyberspace, do away altogether with the designation "Southern" and stop worrying about literary classifications grounded in place and region? As a professor of Southern Studies, I certainly would not want to endorse this last idea, for self-preservation if nothing else, but in today's critical climate regionalism is by and large neglected as an issue for discussion. As Kowalewski observes, "the critical assumption seems to be that region or 'a sense of place' is not an imaginative factor that can be internalized and struggled with in the same literarily rewarding ways that writers struggle with issues of race, class, and gender."[4] One thing I hope to do in this book is to suggest otherwise.

There are no easy answers to these questions about regional classification, and the fact that there are not suggests that Western fiction by Southerners fundamentally challenges the generally accepted parameters of what we designate as "Southern" and more generally as "regional" fiction. Quite simply, contemporary Southern literature about the West represents a startling break in the Southern literary tradition, and it is this break I explore here, focusing on what this literary development suggests not only about the nature of contemporary Southern — and Western — literature and identity but also about the cultural myths shaping America's conception of itself.

Some literary history and cultural context — Southerners never want to stray too far from history — may help illuminate the significance of the contemporary developments. Traditionally, Southern literature has been firmly grounded in a strong sense of place, and that place has been the South, particularly the small town and the countryside.[5] The literature of the Southern literary renaissance — that is,

works written from approximately 1920 until right after World War II
— for the most part explores Southern life in these settled places with
an emphasis on individuals making do, or not making do, in tightly
knit Southern communities. Fiction in the classic American tradition,
or at least what was once deemed classic — Herman Melville, James
Fennimore Cooper, Henry David Thoreau, Ernest Hemingway, and
a few others — tends to celebrate a solitary hero breaking out *from* a
restrictive society and *into* a world of uncharted freedom. Southern
fiction, however, tends to celebrate those who do not leave the community but integrate themselves into it, while still maintaining their
individuality and dignity — that is, without being completely subsumed by the community.

A solitary figure breaking free from the community would, in the
fiction of most Southern writers, be less a hero than a potential psy-
chopath, a person tragically alone and isolated, cut off from the nour-
ishing bonds of family and community. Perhaps the most frightening
depiction of this pattern exists in Cormac McCarthy's *Child of God*,
which portrays the devolution of a yeoman farmer into something
close to a primate when he is evicted from his land; he ends up living
in a cave — becoming a "caveman" — and sleeping with the corpses of
his murder victims. If the American pioneer hero sets out in a straight
line away from society and into the wilderness, the Southern hero typically stays, establishes his or her position within society, and shores
up — rather than breaks free from — the boundaries separating culture from wilderness. Drawing on a popular image from Westerns, one
can understand American society — in very simple terms, of course —
as a wagon train moving progressively west. Southern society, on the
other hand, is the walled fort the wagon train leaves behind.

Southerners' strong sense of place underlies a striking geographical reorientation that took place during the 1920s and 1930s in terms

of Southern identity. Before that time, Southerners characteristically used a north-south orientation to define themselves, with the North and all it stood for (Yankees, industrialism, urbanism, and so on) standing opposed to the South and "Southernness" (the Southern belle and gentleman, agrarian life, leisure, and the like). But in the 1920s, a number of Southern writers shifted from a north-south to an east-west orientation, with the South now aligned as the East, characteristically described as a version of the settled society of premodern Europe, and with the North as the West, a manifestation of the forces of rapacious expansion, which was viewed geographically as imperialist exploration and discovery and viewed economically as industrial capitalism.

Nowhere is this geocultural shift more clear than in the work of the Nashville Agrarians, particularly in their 1930 symposium *I'll Take My Stand*. Although it is anything but a unified work, with its twelve contributors taking their own individual stands, most of the writers—as they acknowledge in book's opening section, "Introduction: A Statement of Principles"—"tend to support a Southern way of life against what may be called the American or prevailing way; and all as much as agree that the best terms in which to represent the distinction are contained in the phrase, Agrarian *versus* Industrial."[6] Broadly speaking, the cultural opposition "Agrarian *versus* Industrial" breaks down something like this: Agrarian cultures are leisurely, nonacquistive, backward-looking (their codes and values being derived from history and tradition), and community-based, and they are always grounded in the soil—specifically in agriculturally based economies but more generally in their organic growth from and adaptations to specific locales. Industrial cultures, in contrast, are fast-paced, acquisitive, forward-looking (their codes and values being derived not from history and tradition but from doctrines of progress and expansion), and individual-based, and they are completely cut off from the soil—economies of finance capitalism exploit and commodify property and place, reducing them to abstract units of value.

None of the Agrarians was a trained economist, though a few dabbled in the field when critics deemed them hopeless romantics and worse. Not surprisingly, then, their calls for an Agrarian society are based less on rigorous number crunching and economic analysis than on rhetorical strategies defending the traditional and attacking the modern. Here is where the east-west orientation comes in, as several of the Agrarians go to great lengths to establish the South as an embodiment of settled society linked with forces of the East—that is, eastern settlement as opposed to western expansion. A characteristic Agrarian analysis establishes the South as less American than European—not reflecting the Europe of the 1920s and 1930s, then in the throes of postwar upheaval and en route to a new war, but premodern, traditional Europe. How far back into the European past the Agrarians go to find their model depends on their subject: for politics, it is pre-French Revolution; for religion, pre-Reformation; for economics, precapitalism.

In "Reconstructed But Unregenerate," John Crowe Ransom writes that "the South is unique on this continent for having founded and defended a culture which was according to the European principles of culture," explaining that the Europe of which he speaks is "the core of unadulterated Europeanism, with its self-sufficient, backward-looking, intensively provincial communities" (ITMS 3, 5). Allen Tate works the same idea in "Remarks on the Southern Religion," arguing that while the rest of America—and modern Europe, too—cut itself off from traditional European life by embracing a radical progressivism, the South stuck with its traditionalism and so *became* Europe. Speaking specifically of the Old South, Tate writes that "the South could be ignorant of Europe because it *was* Europe; that is to say, the South had taken root in native soil. And the South could remain simple-minded because it had no use for the intellectual agility required to define its position. Its position was self-sufficient and self-evident; it was European where the New England position was self-conscious and colonial" (ITMS 171).

As Tate suggests, using an argument he had developed a year earlier in his biography of Jefferson Davis, the split between the North and the South that eventually led to the Civil War is best understood actually as a conflict between East and West:

> The War between the States has a remote origin, and it cannot be understood apart from the chief movements of European history since the Reformation. It was another war between America and Europe, and "America," in the second great attempt, won. The South was the last stronghold of European civilization in the western hemisphere, a conservative check upon the restless expansiveness of the industrial North, and the South had to go. . . . The War between the States was the second and decisive struggle of the Western spirit against the European—the spirit of restless aggression against a stable spirit of ordered economy—and the Western won.[7]

The Agrarians in 1930 found the Western spirit of restless aggression once again threatening the South, this time in the form of industrialism and its most terrifying manifestation—the modern industrial state.

Industrialism was a modern-day manifestation of the pioneering spirit that in pushing ever westward first undid traditional societies in Europe and then later those of America. It is this pioneering spirit that Allen Tate laments in his great poem "The Mediterranean." The poet, enjoying a serene and quietly magical picnic on the Mediterranean, suddenly thinks of the destructive forces of exploration that drove men to set sail beyond the sea on which he looks out:

> What country shall we conquer, what fair land
> Unman our conquest and locate our blood?
> We've cracked the hemispheres with careless hand!
> Now from the Gates of Hercules we flood
> Westward, westward.[8]

Rather than seeing explorers and pioneers as heroic figures of manifest destiny, as did most Americans of the day, the Agrarians found them to be the embodiment of selfish individualism, destructive expansionism, and never-satisfied wanderlust—the embodiment, that is, of what they derogatorily deemed "progress." Industrialism, as John Crowe Ransom writes, "is the contemporary form of pioneering; yet since it never consents to define its goal, it is a pioneering on principle, and with an accelerating speed." Ransom describes industrialism sundering the bonds of family and community: "Industrialism is an insidious spirit, full of false promises and generally fatal to establishments since, when it once gets into them for a little renovation, it proposes never again to leave them in peace. Industrialism is rightfully a menial, of almost miraculous cunning but no intelligence; it needs to be strongly governed or it will destroy the economy of the household. Only a community of tough conservative habit can master it" (ITMS 15–16). Ransom and the other Agrarians of course hoped that the South would embrace precisely this "community of tough conservative habit" in order to resist industrialism.

Despite their allegiance to European models of conservative community, the Agrarians for a while dreamed of teaming up with like-minded regionalists from the American West, with whom they shared a fundamental conviction that the South and the West were colonies of the North and the forces of finance capitalism. Moreover, the Agrarians occasionally turned to the West for rhetorical models to endorse regionalism; unlike most Americans, however, who looked west to celebrate America's manifest destiny, the Agrarians embraced the resistance to American expansionism, lionizing instead Native Americans and their efforts to stop America's westward progression. Native Americans, by the Agrarians' regionalist model, were obvious victims of the same pioneering spirit from which they saw Dixie suffering. John Crowe Ransom, for instance, begins one of his most important essays on regionalism, "The Aesthetics of Regionalism," with a description of bustling Indian pueblos he saw on a trip to New Mexico. Ransom marvels at what he perceives as the Indians' community spirit and order, concluding that what he witnessed "was regionalism; flourishing on the meanest capital, surviving stubbornly, and brilliant. In the face of the efforts of the insidious white missions and the aggressive government schools to 'enlighten' these Indian people, their culture persists, though for the most part it goes back to the Stone Age, and they live as they always have lived."[9]

Ransom then relates a story of a chief's refusal to accept relief money from the federal government because he believed the influx of cash would corrupt traditional folkways and structures. For Ransom this adamant chief, embracing beliefs close to his own as philosophical regionalist, is a hero who refuses to degrade the aesthetics of culture for short-term economic gain. Ransom concludes his discussion of Native Americans with a paean to Indian nobility. After noting their hardheaded pride and their disdain for white culture, Ransom writes:

Noble with a more positive merit too, for Indians lead a life which has an ancient pattern, and has been perfected a long time, and is conscious of the weight of tradition behind it; compared with which the pattern of life of the white men in that region, parvenus as they are, seems improvised and lacking in dignity. And noble because the Indians make their life precisely what it is, in every particular, whereas life for the white men depends on what they can buy with their money, and they buy from everybody, including the Indian. The superiority of Indians, by which term the philosophical spectator refers to their obviously fuller enjoyment of life, lies in their regionalism.[10]

What odd brothers-in-arms, sophisticated aesthete John Crowe Ransom and Native Americans of the Southwest. Of course, Ransom never sought to align the Agrarians with the Native Americans in any way other than rhetorically, but he did find the icon of the Noble Savage useful for celebrating traditional culture and attacking the modern spirit. The romanticism both of the image and of Ransom's invocation of it needs no further comment.

Other Southern writers from the 1930s and 1940s likewise invoked the Noble Savage and Native American culture—obviously associated with the West but not the Westering spirit—as rebukes to modern society and the breakdown of traditional culture by the forces of westward-moving progress. In Faulkner's *Go Down, Moses* (1942), for instance, Ike McCaslin, inspired by his Native American mentor, Sam Fathers, repudiates his inheritance and place within family and community to live a life replicating the ascetic simplicity and purity of the premodern Native Americans. To Ike's eyes, the life embodied in Sam Fathers, based on timeless rituals of the hunt and of the cycles of nature, is ethically and morally pure, free from the sins of Southern history, particularly slavery and exploitation of the land. "Sam Fathers set me free," Ike says at one point.[11] Ike may not go literally west—he continues to live in Jefferson—but he does go to the West imaginatively, believing he has found a wilderness space free from the corruption undermining traditional Southern society, a space where he can stand tall as a paragon of virtue and a guiding light to others. Following a logic close to that which Donald Worster sees as underlying Frederick Jackson Turner's thesis concerning the frontier's shaping of the American identity, Ike patterns his life according to the ways of the wilderness, hoping that he will be thus restored to a state of innocence.[12] In his unbounded hopefulness, Ike even dreams of his family and Southern society's being restored as well through his acts.

In Ransom's eyes, Ike would probably be a regionalist hero, a figure similar to his Native American chief, but things are never so simple in Faulkner. Despite Ike's nobility, Faulkner makes it clear that his actions are ultimately misguided and irresponsible, a shirking of duty that contributes to his family's and his community's decline—a fact made clear in "Delta Autumn," where everything Ike stands for is coming, or has already come, completely undone. In Faulkner's world the burdens of history are the responsibilities of history, and they must be faced up to and dealt with. Not to do so, to believe that one can step outside history and responsibility—to go imaginatively west—is to live in a fanciful dream world, one similar to Ike's vision of himself and the wilderness existing forever in "a dimension free of both time and space."[13]

Despite its irresponsible escapism, Ike's vision of a simpler life, drawn according to Native American patterns, nonetheless remains a powerful commentary on the breakdown of traditional life and the decline of the heroic in modern society, much as Ransom's description of the Native American pueblo does. That Ike's idealism is powerless and irrelevant in the modern South—while he dreams of an eternal wilderness, loggers are progressively cutting down the woods

—suggests both his misguided understanding of modernity and modernity's misguided notions of "progress." Ike's position as noble hunter mirrors the positions of Old Ben, the great bear, and Sam Fathers, the Native American; all three are heroes from previous ages, out of place in the contemporary world of piddling souls and capitalist enterprise demonstrated most clearly in the construction of the railroads and the logging of the forests. All three are doomed to destruction and irrelevance. That does not make Ike any less admirable as an embodiment of a life based on respect for and commitment to the natural world, the doctrine expressed in the sacred rituals of the hunt that Sam Fathers has taught him and by which Ike has patterned his life.

An even more dramatic invocation of Native American traditionalism in order to rebuke modern notions of society and progress comes in Caroline Gordon's *Green Centuries* (1941). Set in eighteenth-century North Carolina, the novel follows the exploits of two brothers, Archy and Orion Outlaw, who flee west to begin new lives after taking part in a Regulator ambush of British soldiers. Archy and Orion appear to have all the trappings of classic American frontier heroes: active participants in the manifest destiny of America, they battle the British, push west to open up new territories, and wage war with the Native Americans. But Gordon drastically undermines the paradigm of the frontier hero and westward expansionism. Archy's capture by and then assimilation into a Cherokee tribe reveals that American Indian culture is anything but savage; indeed, structured by religious beliefs and traditional folkways, the Cherokee civilization *is* the only civilization on the frontier. The culture of the white settlements, in contrast, always threatens to collapse into barbarism, and sometimes does, because the fundamental bonds of civilized life are repeatedly

torn asunder by the restlessness and individualism of the frontiersmen
— men who, unable to root themselves in a particular place, time and
again pull up stakes to head deeper into the wilderness.

Orion is just such a man, but it is not until the end of the novel that
he understands the destruction wreaked by his perpetual movement.
After participating in an Indian massacre in which Archy is killed
and returning to find his wife on her deathbed, Orion comes to see
that his insatiable drive west has destroyed both his own life and the
lives of his loved ones. Here are his thoughts, as he looks up at the con-
stellation from which he takes his name, seeing in the stars "the
hunter's foot, his club, his girdle, the red eye of the bull that he pur-
sued ever westward":

> His father had come west across the ocean, leaving all that he cared
> about behind. And he himself as soon as he had grown to manhood
> had looked at the mountains and could not rest until he knew what
> lay beyond them. But it seemed that a man had to flee farther each
> time and leave more behind him and when he got to the new place
> he looked up and saw Orion fixed upon his burning wheel, always
> pursuing the bull but never making the kill. Did Orion will any
> longer the westward chase? No more than himself. Like the
> mighty hunter he had lost himself in the turning. Before him lay
> the empty west, behind him the loved things of which he was
> made. . . . Were not men raised into the westward turning stars only
> after they had destroyed themselves? [14]

Although unstated here, certainly a newfound awareness of the value
of being settled, of creating a place, underlies Orion's vision of his
and his namesake's undoing. To the west lies emptiness; to the east,
home and community. Orion's repeated removes deeper into the

empty wilderness, he now sees, have emptied him of his humanity, sundering the ties that once united him with others in love and responsibility.

Like Gordon's works, almost all the literature of the Southern literary renaissance is so powerfully grounded in a sense of place that movement itself—in whatever direction, but particularly westward—is characteristically viewed with distrust and suspicion. A Southerner's nightmare might be Gertrude Stein's characterization of America: "Conceive a space that is filled with moving"; and the ongoing Northern bias against the South no doubt in part rests in the Southern celebration of place, Americans associating freedom above all with mobility.[15] A Southern sense of place, of course, implies not mobility but stasis; one can only celebrate place if one is "in place"—that is, settled and rooted. Eudora Welty speaks for a generation of writers in her classic essay "Place in Fiction," in which she explores how place shapes not only literature but also, more generally, consciousness: "If place does work upon genius, how does it? It may be that place can focus the gigantic, voracious eye of genius and bring its gaze to point. Focus then means awareness, discernment, order, clarity, insight—they are like the attributes of love. The act of focusing itself has beauty and meaning; it is the act that, continued in, turns into meditation, into poetry. Indeed, as soon as the least of us stands still, that is the moment something extraordinary is seen to be going on in the world."[16]

Standing still, staying put, putting down roots: such are the means to participate and to draw from the mystery of place. As Welty suggests, place and consciousness are in continuous dialogue and interplay; place interpenetrates and shapes human emotion while human emotion and perception continually reshape place's significance. "Location pertains to feeling; feeling profoundly pertains to place,"

Welty writes; "place in history partakes of feeling, as feeling about history partakes of place."[17] "A sheltered life can be a daring life as well," Welty writes at the end of *One Writer's Beginnings.* "For all serious daring starts from within."[18] There are plenty of journeys in Welty's fiction, but the most significant of these are internal. Welty's most triumphant heroes are brave-hearted characters on imaginative rather than spatial quests, rooted rather than uprooted. "It is through place that we put out roots, wherever birth, chance, fate or our traveling selves set us down," Welty writes in "Place in Fiction," "but where those roots reach toward—whether in America, England or Timbuktu—is the deep and running vein, eternal and consistent and everywhere purely itself, that feeds and is fed by the human understanding."[19] To be in constant motion is to experience only surfaces; to remain in place is to plumb depths.

The Southern opposition between place and movement might also be understood as the opposition between place and time, between the circle of society and the straight line of time—a line always pushing into the future and ushering in change. Carl Degler appropriately entitles his important study of the continuity of Southern history *Place over Time,* his central point being that Southerners have long valued stability and continuity, which are exemplified in an unchanging place, over instability and discontinuity, which are exemplified in a forward-looking time line.[20] Lucinda MacKethan also has noted the Southern resistance to time, explaining that Southerners have long been associated with "an ideology that exalts a sense of place in order to resist time and progress. Time and progress belong to the world outside, or so the myth goes; on the plantations or in the small, sleepy southern towns that are the popular images of the South, time is held back by the places themselves."[21]

Perhaps no one has expressed the Southern tension between time and place better than Robert Penn Warren, who in *All the King's Men* describes the everyday social dynamics of a small town: "In a town like Mason City the bench in front of the harness shop is—or was twenty years ago before the concrete slab got laid down—the place where Time gets tangled in its own feet and lies down like an old hound and gives up the struggle. . . . Time and motion cease to be. It is like sniffing ether, and everything is sweet and sad and far away." [22] Warren's words here not only capture the power of Southern towns to resist time and change but also suggest the dangers inherent in that power. To stop time and motion is to live outside time—that is, outside the workings of historical change and development. As Warren says, it is like sniffing ether. It is like living in a fanciful dream world, similar to Ike McCaslin's dream of hunting in an eternal wilderness. Appropriately enough then, almost every time Jack Burden, the central figure of *All the King's Men*, confronts a crisis he cannot handle, he retreats to his bed for weeks of endless sleep—what he calls the Great Sleep. In hibernating, Jack hopes the world will pass him by, just as "sleepy" Southern towns withdraw into themselves to resist incursions from a changing world.

Jack has another strategy for freeing himself from pressing problems and responsibilities: he flees west. When his discovery of Anne Stanton's affair with Willie sends him into an emotional tailspin, her actions betraying his ideal of Southern womanhood, he immediately hits the road: "When you don't like it where you are you always go west," he says. "We have always gone west" (AKM 309). For Jack, the West is "the end of History" (311); that is, space unburdened by history, space where a person can begin anew, leaving the past behind. At the heart of the West, Jack says, is the dream of the Great Twitch, a belief that defines life as being entirely biologically determined, human activity understood merely as electrical responses between nerves, synapses, and muscles. In its biological determinism, the Great Twitch frees a person from any responsibility for anything that he or she does, and for Jack that freedom is wondrously liberating:

> [The Great Twitch] was the dream that all life is but the dark heave of the blood and the twitch of the nerve. When you flee as far as you can flee, you will always find that dream, which is the dream of our age. At first, it is always a nightmare and horrible, but in the end it may be, in a special way, rather bracing and tonic. At least, it was so for me for a certain time. It was bracing because after the dream I felt that, in a way, Anne Stanton did not exist. The words *Anne Stanton* were simply a name for a peculiarly complicated piece of mechanism which should mean nothing whatsoever to Jack Burden, who himself was simply another rather complicated piece of mechanism. At that time, when I first discovered that view of things — really discovered, in my own way and not from any book—I felt that I had discovered the secret source of all strength and all endurance. That dream solves all problems. (AKM 311)

The Great Twitch may temporarily solve Jack's ethical and moral problems but it does so by obliterating ethics and morality. It is a tactic at the other extreme from that of the Great Sleep, the dream of the traditional South, which stops time and motion by celebrating a world of unchanging tradition. The Great Twitch, the dream of the West, destroys the past by embracing experience as endless motion in an eternal present.

In the end, Jack realizes that he must put aside both the Great Sleep and the Great Twitch. He recognizes both the dangers in wallowing in the past as if there is no present (geoculturally, the South) and the dangers in moving freely about in the present as if there is no past (geoculturally, the West). He knows he must somehow live on the border between these two dreams, or these two regions, drawing from both so that he remains aware not only of history but also of change and development, aware not only of individual freedom but also of community and commitment to others. As he says at the novel's close, he and Anne, now married, must leave the family home (here emblematic of the closing off and turning inward of the Southern imagination) and "go into the convulsion of the world, out of history into history and the awful responsibility of Time" (AKM 438). They must, in other words, depart from a place stagnating in history and move into the ever-changing historical present, accepting the burden not only of the past but also of the present.

This is precisely the lesson that Katherine Anne Porter underscores in her stories about Miranda, particularly in "Old Mortality" and "Pale Horse, Pale Rider." At the end of "Old Mortality," the eighteen-year-old Miranda is about to bolt from her family and her husband to start a new life. As we learn in "Pale Horse, Pale Rider," she heads west, settling in Denver. Miranda is sick and tired of what she finds to be the smothering bonds of family; she is particularly burdened by the overwhelming power of her family's history, endlessly told in stories by her elders, to diminish the present and determine the future. "It is I who have no place," Miranda declares, expressing her belief that she no longer has a role in the family because of her desires for autonomy and independence. As she looks upon her father and her aunt chatting merrily together (and ignoring her), Miranda proclaims her rebellion: "*I will be free of them, I shall not even remember them.*" [23]

Miranda here expresses the dream of the West — a dream of starting over in a world wiped clean of history, of embracing the joy, wonder, and possibility found in a present unburdened by the past and one's own memories. Porter emphasizes that Miranda's liberating dream of living as an amnesiac is every bit as romantic and unreasonable as the sentimental stories relished by her family. Miranda's dream of complete individual freedom, of living free from any confining ties, expresses not only her arrogance and pride but also her childishness. The story's final sentence drives home the immaturity underlying her optimism: "At least I can know the truth about what happens to me, she assured herself silently, making a promise to herself, in her hopefulness, her ignorance" (CSP 221).

Three years later and living in Denver, Miranda in "Pale Horse, Pale Rider" still dreams of living as an amnesiac, though she is learning how difficult being adrift can be — though, in fact, she is not really adrift. While she is no longer tied down by her family (except when she's asleep and dreaming), many demanding people crush in upon her. So burdened does she feel that at one point she breaks down, saying in despair and not hopefulness, "I wish I could lose my memory and forget my own name" (CSP 289). Miranda eventually succumbs to the hopelessness — rather than to the imagined hopefulness — underpinning her dream of radical individual freedom: rather than liberating her from society's constraints and paving the way for her fulfillment, her dream isolates and alienates her, closing down the future and pushing her toward becoming one of the bitter and wayward individuals who inhabit her world, people she characterizes as "speechless animals" (291). Utterly alienated at the end of the story, Miranda feels displaced merely by being alive, merely by having a body. "The body is a curious monster, no place to live in, how could anyone feel at home there?" she thinks (CSP 313). The narrator, describing how far Miranda has fallen away from the human community, comments that "her hardened, indifferent heart shuddered in despair of itself, because before it had been tender and capable of love" (315). For Miranda to achieve fulfillment, she must somehow discover a balance between what she says are the "tough filaments of memory and hope pulling taut backwards and forwards" (304), a balance in which opposing tensions ground her in the past and the future, in memories and desires, in place and space—in other words, in "the awful responsibility of Time" that Warren's Jack Burden embraces at the end of *All the King's Men* (438).[24]

A similar oppositional interplay between the South and the West and their imaginative manifestations—place and space, community and individualism, despair and hope, standing still and moving about, an unchanging past and the eternal present, and so on—can be found in much of the writing of the Southern literary renaissance. While many traditionalist authors, including most of those associated with the Agrarians, privilege one pole of this opposition, virtually suppressing values associated with movement, other writers debate these issues more complexly. As Warren and Porter do, most of these writers look toward the borders of the two regions, if not literally then metaphorically, aware of the dangers of either extreme. Even Welty, the Southern writer perhaps most celebratory of the importance of place and placement, characteristically seeks to reconcile conflicting urges to stay put and to wander, exploring the dynamics between rooting oneself solidly in the community and lighting out from it. In Welty's fiction, the worship of place always threatens to harden into uncritical provinciality, destructive in its stasis and inertia. This sort of provinciality can be seen most obviously in all those ladies in her stories who flit about "policing" social mores and etiquette—the three women in "Lilly Daw and the Three Ladies," the womenfolk of Morgana in *The Golden Apples*, and the elderly women of Mount Salus in *The Optimist's Daughter*, for example. These characters dedicate themselves to defending the cultural borders of their societies from outside encroachment and to maintaining damage control when such encroachment occurs, as it does in *The Optimist's Daughter* when

Fay (who is appropriately a Westerner, from Texas) marries Judge McKelva and moves dead center into Mount Salus society.

Opposed to those who blindly uphold the status quo and tradition are Welty's wanderers—those who undertake journeys, literal and imaginative, beyond the borders of society and the socially acceptable. Always associated with movement and the crossing of borders, these wanderers are frequently associated specifically with the West and with westward movement. In "Shower of Gold," for instance, King MacLain's wanderings become the stuff of town legend, a legend of Western sunsets and golden horizons. "I believe he's been to California," Fate Rainey says of King, voicing the local myth. "Don't ask me why. But I picture him there. I see King in the West, out where it's gold and all that."[25] And when King returns to Morgana and lurks about trying to see his wife, Snowdie, Fate characterizes the town's efforts to keep him away from her, and thus out of his influence: "We shut the West out of Snowdie's eyes of course" (GA 14).

There's much that is undeniably glorious about King and those other "golden" figures who wander throughout Welty's fiction. They are independent and free-spirited, everywhere flaunting convention and restraint, characteristically through a joyous and uninhibited sensuality. They strive to live as intensely as possible. In "The Wanderers," Virgie Rainey, herself a wanderer, characterizes the driving force of King—and by implication, those like him—as that of a goat butting "against the wall he would not agree to himself or recognize. What fortress indeed would ever come down, except before hard little horns, a rush and a stampede of the pure wish to live?" (GA 264). As does King, the wanderers radiate a golden aura, a grandeur of spirit. "He looked like the preternatural month of June," the narrator of "Sir Rabbit" says of King (GA 107); and in "Shower of Gold," when Snowdie announces that she is pregnant by King, she glows with a radiance he has passed to her. "It was like a shower of something had struck her," Fate Rainey says of Snowdie, "like she'd been caught out in something bright. It was more than the day" (GA 7).

And yet for all their vitality and independence, the wanderers remain just that—wanderers, adrift in the world, restless and unsatisfied, incapable of nurturing long-term, meaningful relationships with others and of rooting themselves to a particular place. The narrator's characterization of Miss Eckhart and Virgie Rainey, two wanderers in "June Recital," suggests both their freedom and their sufferings: "Both Miss Eckhart and Virgie Rainey were human beings terribly at large, roaming on the face of the earth. And there were others of them— human beings, roaming, like lost beasts" (GA 96). Miss Eckhart's and Virgie's fierce independence clearly comes at a dear cost, a separateness forcing them to roam "like lost beasts." Welty's wanderers remain fundamentally alone, outside of a nurturing community, and thus have little to shield them from their loneliness and separateness. Those of large spirit, like Virgie and King, suffer grandly, passionately embracing their imaginative dreams at whatever cost; those of lesser spirit—such as King's sons Eugene and Ran, who are haunted by their father's wanderlust but lack his joyous and glorious passion— suffer mightily, unable to be happy wandering or settling into place.

Can one indeed be a settled wanderer? Eugene's and Ran's failures suggest the tremendous difficulty of reconciling these conflicting impulses, but other characters in Welty's fiction are more successful. Rather than the stay-at-homes (and I mean that literally and imaginatively) or the wanderers (roaming about, unconnected to place), Welty's true heroes and heroines are those who somehow do both, living both "placed" and "at large." One such figure is Cassie Morrison in *The Golden Apples*, a sensitive young woman who, though not so creatively rebellious and inspired as Virgie and the other wanderers, is more reflective and observant than they—that is, more at home in the world and more focused. As Louis Rubin observes, Cassie "possesses the vision that understands what lies in and under the surfaces of her experience without at the same time being so driven and distracted by that knowledge that she cannot live in a place."[26]

While Cassie stays in her hometown and wanders imaginatively, another of Welty's heroines, Laurel McKelva in *The Optimist's Daughter*, who has lived away from her hometown, Mount Salus, for years, decides at the end not to move back there after her father's death but to return to her life in Chicago. Laurel knows she no longer has a vital place in her hometown, despite what her friends say; her return to the Midwest—suggesting the balance between East and West—affirms her desire to carry on with her life in *her* place. She is taking flight at the end of the book, escaping the nets of Mount Salus, more focused, aware, and alive to the world about her. Like Jack Burden in *All the King's Men*, Laurel leaves the small town of her upbringing, forgoing a world of unchanging history for the historical present, forging a new life in a place of her own making.

All of the writers from the Southern literary renaissance whom we have briefly discussed—John Crowe Ransom, Allen Tate, William Faulkner, Caroline Gordon, Robert Penn Warren, Katherine Anne Porter, and Eudora Welty—work with the interplay of place and movement, of the settled nature of the Southern community and the restlessness of the wanderer, be it the pioneer heading west or a modern manifestation of the frontiersman/woman striking out toward new territories, imaginative and otherwise. Metaphorically this interplay embodies the opposition between place and space, the

East and the West, history and the eternal present—crucial themes, as I have suggested, in the literature of the Southern literary renaissance. How the writers portray and work with the interplay of place and movement varies, of course, in tone and emphasis. John Crowe Ransom, for example, is much more damning of movement to the West than Welty is, despite the fact that no one celebrates a sense of place more fully than she. But whatever their differences in emphasis, almost all writers of the Southern literary renaissance underscore the significance exerted by place in the development of individual and communal identity. Even when pointing out the dangers sometimes found in uncritically accepting place and tradition, writers of the renaissance never stray too far from celebrating the healing and wondrous power of a settled life, of a life "in place." Place counts in the Southern literary imagination; there is no getting free of it, or at least, there is no getting free of it and remaining healthy and whole. Wendell Berry speaks for scores of Southern writers when he says that "if you don't know where you are, you don't know who you are." [27]

But what of writers coming after the renaissance, those writing from the 1950s and afterward? Although it would be hard to prove absolutely, I think it is fair to say that since the end of World War II, with the South developing into a much more prosperous and urban, and suburban, region—the Cotton Belt having become the Sun Belt—the significance of place has been losing its importance in the Southern imagination. This is not to say that Southern writers are no longer portraying Southern characters in Southern settings—of course they are. But it is to suggest that these writers by and large are not stressing the mysteries of place and the value of being rooted as strongly as the earlier ones did, nor are they focusing so much on the uniqueness of the Southern scene and on the power of specific locales to shape identity.

The contrast between the following observations by Eudora Welty and Walker Percy suggests the shift that is occurring. Welty once said that the inexhaustible subject of her fiction is the simple expression "you and me, here."[28] The statement emphasizes the importance of place in the interactions between people; it is not merely "you and me" but "you and me in a particular place." On the other hand, Walker Percy—perhaps the most important of the postwar Southern writers and a good friend of Welty's—liked to say that his fiction has nothing fundamentally to do with a particular place, and he meant most particularly the South. In Percy's view, his fiction explores universal existential problems, examining matters that are applicable to anyone, at any time, at any place; it just happens to be set in the South. Percy's analysis, although no doubt overstating the insignificance of place in his work, nonetheless points to an important reconfiguration of the Southern literary imagination.

The diminishment of place as a shaping and creative force in the Southern literary imagination points to a postwar cultural trend found not only in the South but also in the rest of America: regional identity is waning.[29] Although Americans may still distinguish themselves regionally, that identification nowadays seems willed and self-conscious, less an instinctive feeling than a deliberate choice. There are any number of reasons for the diminishing influence of place in the creation of local identity and culture: people move more often (on the average, once every four years), travel more and farther, live in urban and suburban developments that look fundamentally the same all over America, watch the same television programs, listen to the same music, move easily about in cyberspace, eat the same fast food in establishments that are exact copies of each other. In other words, most Americans live and work in essentially the same cultural system, and so they are less tied to and grounded in one particular place.

The titles of two studies in technology and society suggest the down-playing of place and groundedness in postmodern culture: McKenzie Wark's *Virtual Geography: Living with Global Media Events* (Indiana University Press, 1994) and Joshua Meyrowitz's *No Sense of Place: The Impact of Electronic Media on Social Behavior* (Oxford University Press, 1985). This diminishment of place exists also on a larger scale and is clearly part of a worldwide trend. Every day we hear terms suggestive of the breakdown of geographic cultural borders — "the global economy," "multinational corporations," "the global village." Anyone following the stock market lately knows how bound together national economies have become; the devaluation of the Thai currency in 1997 began a ripple effect that for several years shook the entire world financial system. Wayne Franklin and Michael Steiner, noting the antispatial bias in postmodern culture, call this condition "spatial amnesia."[30]

Contemporary Southern writers have not been immune to this amnesia, though I would guess that overall they probably have resisted it a bit more strongly than other American authors. Richard Gray is no doubt correct in arguing that changes in material culture occur much more dramatically and more quickly than those in mind and imagination — old patterns can live on even in a culture of strip malls — but certainly we are beginning to see telling effects in contemporary Southern writing.[31] In part because of the sociological changes just noted and in part because of the influence of developments in postmodern literature — a literature, broadly speaking, celebrating imaginative free play rather than memory — Southern writers have more and more been striking out on their own, moving away from the imaginative shape of "classic" Southern literature that is so secure in regional place, history, and memory. Even if the type of pyrotechnic postmodern literature exemplified by the writing of Thomas Pynchon and Robert Coover has not taken deep root in the South (the works of Donald Barthelme and John Barth are notable exceptions), certainly postmodern culture is pushing Southern writers, as Julius Rowan Raper notes, toward a literature less classically Southern in shape and texture—one that relies less on matters of regional life than, in Raper's words, on issues of "philosophy, mythology, and post-Freudian psychology."[32]

Not surprisingly, then, we are now seeing a much more diverse literature emerging from the South, one that is traveling much further afield in terms of subject, setting, and technique. Certainly there are a number of authors who still write what we might call traditional Southern fiction, works delving into a Southern sense of place, history, community, and family. The novel of the Southern dysfunctional family, for instance, continues to be immensely popular—everyone seems to love to read about nutty Southern home life. And as Fred Hobson recently observed in his Lamar Lectures, many African American writers from the South continue to write powerful fiction that for the most part sticks to the classic forms.[33] Nevertheless, there exist a large number of Southern writers who are either abandoning or drastically revising the old forms, and one of the most dramatic developments is their turn to the West.[34] Theirs is a rich and diverse literature, fueled by the creative interplay of the Southern and the Western imaginative landscapes. Transformed by their Western journeys, contemporary Southern writers in turn transform their visions of the South and in the process reconfigure the Southern literary imagination.

2 / Bleeding Westward

Westerns. We have all read and watched them. We all know their appeal. Cowboys, horses, shoot-outs, Indians, majestic landscapes, the lonesome trail. Recent studies of the genre have suggested reasons for its tremendous and ongoing popularity. In *West of Everything: The Inner Life of Westerns,* Jane Tompkins argues that Westerns appeal to "a Wild West of the psyche," which she describes as the psychic hunger for real, hard, down-to-earth experience — "action that totally saturates the present moment, totally absorbs the body and mind, and directs one's life to the service of an unquestioned goal."[1] What stands opposite the Western, and what the Western vision frees us from, is our everyday work and domestic life — our shopping trips to the mall, our bowls of cereal, our answering telemarketers' calls during supper. Westerns posit an unenclosed world free from the nets of culture, a vast, wide-open space where a person survives the elements by acting elementally — by instinct, bravery, and physical prowess.

Not only do Westerns have a timeless appeal, but also, like most forms of popular literature, they have a particular appeal and perform specific cultural work. As Lee Clark Mitchell argues in *Westerns: Making the Man in Fiction and Film*, Westerns have remained so popular because of the genre's "transformational flexibility," its ability to adapt and adjust its formula and parameters according to shifting cultural demands, all the while remaining recognizable as the "Western." "Like other escapist narratives," Mitchell writes, "Westerns map out anxieties about conditions from which people want to escape — anxieties that change with time as do their imaginative solutions. Countless Westerns have appeared for nearly a century now, supposedly fixed by generic code but actually responsive to crises and fears that earlier Westerns failed to anticipate."[2] Mitchell argues persuasively that the central problem that Westerns explore — the glue that holds the genre together — is the construction of masculinity. I would stress that the problem of masculinity is inseparable from larger questions of national identity and purpose, particularly on the level of cultural myth.

While Westerns, all along, have often been written by Easterners, until recently the genre seems to have had little appeal for Southern writers. I cannot think of any significant author from the South who has written a Western, not counting those on the contemporary scene whom I am examining here.[3] There are a number of compelling reasons to suggest why Southern writers have stayed close to home, many of which I have already mentioned: Southern writers have characteristically embraced a strong sense of place (they are more comfortable in a historical place than a timeless space); they have typically cast cold eyes on escapist schemes (there is enough of that in Southern culture and mythology); they did not need to go West to examine problems of masculinity, honor, and violence (what is more Southern than all that?).

But during the last fifteen years or so — and earlier, if you count, as I do, James Dickey's *Deliverance* as a Western — a handful of significant Southern authors have written Westerns. This wild bunch includes Cormac McCarthy, Madison Smartt Bell, Barry Hannah, and Clyde Edgerton. If Mitchell is right that Westerns first and foremost deal with constructions of masculinity, it should come as no surprise that all these writers are male and that their fiction explores men creating and destroying themselves in a West for the most part free from women and culture (though Edgerton, much less of a bad boy, includes in his novel *Redeye* a woman's remaking of herself in the wilderness). Put simply, the West and the genre of the Western let these good ole boys really be boys again — free from the cultural constraints holding back the Southern male.

But of course the situation is not that simple. That male Southern authors have lately been writing Westerns signals far more than anxiety concerning masculinity and domesticity; it also signals anxieties about the origins and construction of postmodern society, particularly the embedded ideologies that define "progress" and civility, and reveals what those ideologies mask and suppress in society's definition of itself. America, as Richard Rodriguez notes in his essay "True West," has from its beginnings been conceived longitudinally, and the myth of the West and westward expansion has in many ways become the myth of America.[4] By writing Westerns, Southerners seek to interrogate that myth — a myth, declares Donald Worster, so overwhelmingly optimistic as to be blinding.[5]

Of course, these Southern authors are not by any means the first to write Westerns that interrogate American culture and ideology. Given the ideologically loaded packaging of the genre, particularly the obvious issues regarding the hero and the confrontation with alien others, all writers of Westerns, it could be argued, participate in this interrogation, though some more deliberately than others. Walter Van Tilburg Clark, to cite only one example of an author who deliberately reworks the genre to explore national issues and problems, portrays the disturbing similarities between vigilante justice and fascism in *The Ox-Bow Incident*. Since the early 1970s, overt manipulation of the genre has become increasingly popular. Postmodernism's delight in subverting forms and genres, exposing their fictionality, has led to the increased popularity of what critics now call "anti-Westerns," works that employ parody and metafictional techniques to comment upon—to revitalize, some would say—the form from contemporary perspectives.[6]

In their interrogation of the American legend of the West, contemporary Southern writers focus primarily on the dark undercurrents typically masked in the optimistic versions of American expansionism, particularly the violent dispersal of Native Americans and the raw capitalistic enterprise that pillaged land and people for profit. Though anything but neo-Agrarians, these Southern writers nonetheless assume a vantage point not unlike that taken by the Agrarians to critique the American legend and America's destructive drive west. In this they bring to bear upon America's progressivist, forward-looking legends what C. Vann Woodward calls "the irony of Southern history," a perspective grounded in the Southern experience of poverty and defeat that stands diametrically opposed to the American legend of unlimited progress and success.[7]

If the Southerners who write Westerns share a vantage point with the Agrarians, they also stand alongside a group known loosely as the "New Western Historians," who since the 1980s have been revising and reinterpreting Western history in an effort to demythologize the legendary West. In their hands, as Gene M. Gressley observes, America's push westward "was not a heroic story at all, but rather a tale of greed, debasement, and exploitation. Failure, not success, was the guidon of the New Western History in depicting western settlement."[8] Or as Patricia Nelson Limerick, one of the most visible and important of the New Western Historians, says, "A clear appraisal of power and its operations in the American West knocks the wind out of innocent visions of historical understanding as the sponsor of tolerance and good nature."[9]

Southern writers of Westerns are best understood within this larger context of revisionist interrogation of American culture and legend. It has been suggested to me that these writers are at heart romantic escapists who shirk their social responsibilities as artists to explore the paradoxes and problems of the South and instead flee westward into fantasy. Regardless how one feels about art and social responsibility, such a comment misses the powerful cultural critique presented in the Westerns written by Southerners. Even if that cultural critique most fully centers on national rather than Southern matters, the regional and the national are integrally intertwined, particularly in these days when the reach of postmodern industrial and technological culture extends deep into all of America. In writing Westerns, Southern authors are not seeking refuge from the problems of postmodern (and Southern) life but are instead seeking vantage points for exploring those problems.

Turning to the West means turning to the frontier, the heartland of America's mythology. As the dangerous zone where borders and boundaries blur, where society is always under construction, where the civilized mixes with the savage, the frontier has been central to America's concept of itself from the very beginnings of colonization, and many of our most important cultural heroes have been frontiersmen, those who have pushed west into the wilderness. There is no better place from which to witness America's ideological construction —

and destruction — at work; and there is no better place from which to critique that ideological enterprise.

All of the Southerners who write Westerns work broadly within the genre's fundamental shape, though often they revise and work against the formula, in the spirit of the anti-Western. Richard Etulain succinctly describes the basic form: "the Western features a courageous hero, often a cowboy or at least a man on horseback, who combats evil by opposing villainous characters or institutions and who establishes (or reestablishes) order, frequently through violent, redeeming acts." [10] In their focus on reclaiming order through violence, Westerns typically follow a narrative sequence that expresses, in Richard Slotkin's evocative phrase, "regeneration through violence":

> The American must cross the border into "Indian country" and experience a "regression" to a more primitive and natural condition of life so that the false values of the "metropolis" can be purged and a new, purified social contract enacted. Although the Indian and the Wilderness are the settler's enemy, they also provide him with the new consciousness through which he will transform the world. The heroes of this myth-historical quest must therefore be "men (or women) who know Indians" — characters whose experiences, sympathies, and even allegiances fall on both sides of the Frontier. [11]

Leslie Fiedler elaborates on the frontier hero's conversion, writing that the archetypal Western deals "with the confrontation in the wilderness of a transplanted WASP and a radically alien other, an Indian — leading either to a metamorphosis of the WASP into something neither White nor Red (sometimes by adoption, sometimes by sheer emulation, but *never* by actual miscegenation), or else to the annihilation of the Indian (sometimes by castration-conversion or penning off into a ghetto, sometimes by sheer murder)." [12] This blurring of the savage and the civilized in the frontier hero — and, more generally, through-out the frontier itself — becomes the primary focus of the Southern writers who write Westerns; all deliberately manipulate the Western's basic formula in order to probe the frontier's contested ideological battleground and the boundaries imposed by the forces of civilization.

Before describing how the formula operates in *Deliverance* (1970), I want to say a few words about considering this novel as a Western. Though Dickey's novel is obviously not a Western in terms of setting, its fundamental plot patterns and thematic concerns make it a clas-sic narrative of the frontier. Moreover, *Deliverance* represents the contemporary Southern writer's first step toward the West and the Western — the step, that is, of writing "Westerns" set in the South. Some Southern writers have followed Dickey's lead, such as Larry Brown, whose novel *Joe*, set in Mississippi, bears striking resemblances to Jack Schaefer's *Shane*. Other writers, the ones I am discussing in this chapter, have looked further west, beyond Dixie's borders, to ex-plore the frontier experience.

At first glance, *Deliverance* appears to conform closely to the classic narrative of frontier regeneration of which Slotkin and Fiedler speak, particularly with regard to Ed, who must stalk and kill a man in the wilderness in order for him and his friends to survive. Ed's chal-lenge — to hunt the man who is hunting them — demands that he ex-ercise skills both of the wilderness (physical prowess) and of civiliza-tion (rational thinking). To get his man, Ed must scale a treacherous cliff, a climb that he makes entirely by instinct and muscle, and then shoot the ambusher with a bow and arrow, an obvious image of In-dian skill. But he also must use his talents as a graphics designer to figure out where the ambusher will be hiding and where he himself must stand to get a shot off. Ed successfully merges the primal and civilized, killing his man and then later guiding the survivors out of the wilderness. Once Lewis's acolyte, Ed emerges as the group leader, not only when the men are on the river but also later when they are questioned about Drew's death. At home in Atlanta, Ed's rejuvenation appears complete: he is now enthusiastic about his art and design work, and he is happy and fulfilled, including in bed, with his wife. He is a new man, happily merging the wilderness with civilization.

Sort of. As Dickey makes clear in the survivors' actions when they are safely off the river, Ed's rejuvenation is neither so simple nor so innocent, if it is even a rejuvenation. To Ed's eyes, his renewal stems from his being more in touch with his primal self; he can now draw from its power and channel it into productive endeavor. He characterizes his remaking as his carrying of the undammed river within him:

> The river and everything I remembered about it became a possession to me, a personal, private possession, as nothing else in my life ever had. Now it ran nowhere but in my head, but there it ran as though immortally. I could feel it—I can feel it—on different places on my body. It pleases me in some curious way that the river does not exist, and that I have it. In me it still is, and will be until I die, green, rocky, deep, fast, slow, and beautiful beyond reality. . . . The river underlies, in one way or another, everything I do.[13]

As hopeful and positive as Ed is here, his words point less to his regeneration than to his rewriting of his frontier experience — a rewriting involving both deliberate forgetting and translating terror into nostalgia. Ed's experience on the river is anything but the soothing massage he characterizes it as in his memory. Indeed, when Ed falls into the river as he descends the cliff, he describes it not as his plunging into the river but as the river's plunging into him: "The river went into my right ear like an ice pick. I yelled, a tremendous walled-in yell, and then I felt the current thread through me, first through my head from one ear and out the other and then complicatedly through my body, up my rectum and out my mouth and also in at the side I was hurt. . . . It had been so many years that I had been really hurt that the feeling was almost luxurious" (D 208). Put simply, Ed is penetrated — raped — by the river, and he enjoys it.

It is precisely this violation that Ed cannot later face, just as Bobby cannot face remembering his literal rape by the mountain man. To escape his past, Bobby flees to Hawaii, as far west as he can go and still be in America, hoping to start completely anew in a place where nobody knows him. Ed, in contrast, stays home and reconfigures his ordeal into nostalgic wistfulness, a nostalgia for the river that no longer exists and thus does not have to be faced again. His reconfiguration also commodifies the river — as he says, it is now his possession — and he creates it into what he wants it to be, noble and serene. Ed's valorized, noble river is a version of America's noble savage, a creation of imperialist nostalgia that idealizes the very thing that the imperialist impulse has destroyed — at the novel's end, the river has been dammed and made into a recreational lake.

Absent, of course, from Ed's nostalgic vision are any thoughts of the two mountain men that he and Lewis have killed. They are safely buried deep beneath the lake, undisturbed and undisturbing, a fitting image both for the violent origins buried deep beneath the surface of American society and for the violent acts now buried deep within Ed's subconscious. Safely back in society and living comfortably in a cultural system with well-defined borders between the civilized and the uncivilized, Ed *must* forget the victims. For him to remember their killing would be to blur this fundamental boundary and to acknowledge what he knows but will not let himself know on the conscious level if he wants to live comfortably and securely: that he is a killer, that he shares a common savagery with the "savages" they have destroyed. It is perhaps this stunning, obliterating knowledge of intimate connection with the man he himself kills that causes Ed to lose consciousness precisely when he lets fly the arrow that penetrates his victim. And it is precisely this knowledge that he represses as he muses about the lake, enjoying the surface and forgetting the bodies—and his connection with them—that lie deep below that surface, just as he "forgets" his homoerotic attraction to Lewis and his fantasies of sexual violation.

Ed, Lewis, and Bobby's rewriting of history to justify themselves and their killings—as Ed says, "we've got to make it unhappen" (D 210)—is a version writ small of the conspiracy of silence repeatedly enacted by America in its march west—a march that in expanding the space of civilization displaces and destroys premodern others (here, the mountain folk who are displaced by the damming of the river) who stand in its way. Ed and his friends' debate on what to do with the body of the man whom Lewis has killed is instructive in this regard. By majority vote, the men decide to hide the body and say nothing about it when they are off the river; that is, by an act embodying one of society's highest ideals—democracy—they decide to undermine the social contract by taking the law into their own hands. When Drew dissents, arguing that "it's not a matter of guts; it's a matter of the law," Lewis responds: "You see any law around here? We're the law. What we decide is going to be the way things are" (D 129–30). Lewis's logic, asserting the validity of whatever "law" is necessary for survival, mirrors that repeatedly used by American society to justify the killing of Native Americans in its expansion westward into new frontiers—the same logic that was conveniently discarded once the settlements were in place and the natives were gone. History was rewritten to cover up society's savagery.

By the "authorized" version of what happened on the river—Ed,

Bobby, and Lewis's version, that is—the events of the novel never actually happened. The canoe trip was just that and nothing more. Drew got killed in an accident. There was no rape; there were no killings. There were not even any mountain men, other than those contracted to drive group's cars back down the river. Events "unhappen" and the novel is erased, just as the stories of Native Americans and everyone else who got in the way during national expansion have been. And with this erasure both Ed—and, more generally, modern society—rest easy, comfortable with the resecured borders between savagery and civilization that were temporarily dismantled by the "unauthorized" version of what happened on that weekend canoe trip down the river.

Like Dickey, Cormac McCarthy explores the violent origins of westward expansion that have been expunged from the national mythology that celebrates the victory of civilization over savagery and the march of progress driving, and justifying, America's manifest destiny. McCarthy's interrogation, like Dickey's, explores the porous borders separating the civilized from the uncivilized, the human from the animal, characteristically in fiction that strips away the veneer of the civilized self, characters devolving toward primal if not bestial identities. Although McCarthy works with these matters in all of his fiction, his Western *Blood Meridian* (1985) is his fullest—and most terrifying—exploration of the brutality underpinning humanity and culture. McCarthy's West is much grimmer and more terrifying than Dickey's. In *Deliverance* Ed and his friends, for all their violent acts, still make reasoned and rational decisions, even if those decisions are for unreasonable and unjust ends. Their journey into the wilderness does not involve becoming entirely bestial; indeed, they remain thoroughly and recognizably human in their killing of "others" and in their later scrambling to whitewash what they have done — and that is Dickey's point about humanity and its masquerade of being "civilized." In *Blood Meridian* there is no masquerade; almost everyone in McCarthy's wilderness is fundamentally bestial, barely recognizable as human.

Becoming bestial is indeed the fate of McCarthy's characters who cross the fragile boundary separating the civilized from the uncivilized, from the settled East into the unsettled West. One of *Blood Meridian*'s epigraphs is a quote from a 1982 issue of the *Yuma Daily Sun* reporting that "a 300,000-year-old fossil skull . . . shows evidence of being scalped." [14] The epigraph's significance for a novel about marauding scalp hunters in the nineteenth century is clear: violence lies at the heart of humankind; it always has, it always will. Because of McCarthy's focus on the elemental nature of humanity, characters who roam about in his West often are described as creatures from primitive, if not prehistoric, times; they are manifestations of our forebears, humanity in its original state. As Glanton and his men are approaching an army outpost, the lieutenant on duty notes their appearance: "Haggard and haunted and blacked by the sun. . . . Even the horses looked alien to any he'd ever seen, decked as they were in human hair and teeth and skin. Save for the guns and buckles and a few pieces of metal in the harness of the animals there was nothing about these arrivals to suggest even the discovery of the wheel" (BM 232).

McCarthy's Western landscape is a vast wasteland, with only a few scattered towns and ranches marking humanity's presence. It is nature at its barest and most fundamental, a "desert absolute . . . devoid of feature" (BM 295). As Charles McGrath has noted, most of McCarthy's novels "describe a world that is, for all intents and purposes, either prehistoric or post-apocalyptic: a barren, hostile place in which civilization — and any recognizable notion of morality — is scarcely discernible." McGrath comments specifically on the blighted landscape of *Blood Meridian*, saying it is "straight out of 'The Road Warrior' — an end-of-the-road stretch in which 'the ragged flames fled down the wind as if sucked by some maelstrom out there in the void, some vortex in that waste apposite to which man's transit and his reckonings alike lay abrogate.'" [15] Indeed, the words "void" and "waste" echo endlessly in McCarthy's descriptions of the blighted landscape in *Blood Meridian*. It is a "shoreless void" (50), "sullen shores of the void" (302), a "void beyond [that] seemed to swallow up [the Kid's] soul" (65). It is "the western rim of the waste" (293), "that cauterized waste" (204), "that immense and bloodslaked waste" (177).

Given the blankness and emptiness of McCarthy's West, the landscape at first glance could perhaps be understood as one of infinite possibility, maybe even a hopeful space for renewal and rebirth, a world clean of history and past failure. As it soon becomes clear, however, McCarthy's Western landscape is, recalling Wallace Stegner's designation, less a "geography of hope" than a geography of terror, uncharted space described as "stark and black and livid like a land of some other order out there whose true geology was not stone but fear" (BM 47). There is no renewal or rebirth in *Blood Meridian*; there are only death and destruction. While people can imaginatively configure the void of the West into whatever order and pattern they desire, that pattern is only a mirage, merely the stuff of dreams — a fantasy that lasts only until someone bigger and stronger comes along to impose a different order.

Although the Judge says that anything is possible in the world, he is not speaking about human potentiality but rather the inexplicableness of the universe, a world whose meaning finally remains totally unfathomable. "Had you not seen it all from birth and thereby bled it of its strangeness it would appear to you for what it is," he says, "a hat trick in a medicine show, a fevered dream, a trance bepopulate with chimeras having neither analogue nor precedent, an itinerant carnival, a migratory tentshow whose ultimate destination after many a pitch in a many a mudded field is unspeakable and calamitous beyond reckoning" (BM 245). If the order people impose on the world is merely the desire for order rather than order itself—as the Judge says, "the order in creation which you see is that which you have put there, like a string in a maze, so that you shall not lose your way" (BM 245)— so too is the belief in creation's mystery merely the desire for that mystery. "Your heart's desire is to be told some mystery," the Judge tells his recruits: "The mystery is that there is no mystery" (252).[16]

In McCarthy's wasteland, all questions of right and wrong, of the ethical and spiritual, are subsumed in the everyday struggle to survive. As the Judge puts it: "Decisions of life and death, of what shall be and shall not, beggar all question of right. In elections of these magnitudes are all lesser ones subsumed, moral, spiritual, natural" (BM 250). According to the Judge—and certainly his commentary holds sway over the novel—there is little to life other than war; all else is merely idle speculation. "War," the Judge says, "is the truest form of divination. It is the testing of one's will and the will of another within that larger will which because it binds them is therefore forced to select. War is the ultimate game because war is at last a forcing of the unity of existence. War is god" (249). War strips the world of all pretense, making it as clean as the desert. The only things remaining are bodies—and blood.

Indeed, in McCarthy's West blood flows everywhere. Blood is the tie that most fundamentally bonds people together—not ties of kinship but ties of killing, of spilling another person's blood. In a world where allegiances shift as easily as wind-blown sand, the only permanent bond is that between killer and victim. "Is not blood the tempering agent in the mortar which bonds?" the Judge asks the Kid (BM 329). Not long after posing this question, the Judge murders the Kid; their bond is now forever sealed.

The American legend proclaims that people move west with hope, purpose, and direction; they want to start over, to feel vital, to remake themselves. There is none of that in *Blood Meridian*, where those heading west are described as "itinerant degenerates bleeding westward like some heliotropic plague" (BM 78), moving ever onward into the "bloodlands of the West" (138). To enter this wasteland is to wander about in unceasing motion, without purpose or direction other than to kill and keep from being killed. As Bernard Schopen has observed, the novel's oft-repeated sentence "They rode on" underscores not only that the scalp hunters are endlessly moving but "that destination is irrelevant, that the only activity of consequence is riding 'on.' So Glanton and his men seem to ride 'to' nowhere, to exist in a present in which the past is meaningless and future imponderable." [17] There is no clear path to anywhere in *Blood Meridian*; at one point, when two parties of men pass each other, they are described as each riding back "the way the other had come, pursuing as all travelers must inversions without end upon other men's journeys" (121).

Is there any sense of settledness, community values, history, home — that is, any sense of established place that stands opposed to the destructive forces everywhere in the novel? Only a few hints. Sprinkled throughout the landscape of *Blood Meridian* are a number of towns and ranches where people live simply and civilly, raising families and performing everyday tasks. McCarthy clearly has a great deal of respect for these people who live with grace and good will, particularly those who master skills and crafts with pride and devotion. The narrator's description of the shotgun Brown carries to the farrier suggests the order and beauty possible in human handiwork that stands in opposition to the chaos manifested in the scalp hunters and their marauding:

> There was a raised center rib between the barrels and inlaid in gold was the maker's name, London. There were two platinum bands in the patent breech and the locks and the hammers were chased with scrollwork cut deeply in the steel and there were partridges engraved at either end of the maker's name there. The purple barrels were welded up from triple skelps and the hammered iron and steel bore a watered figure like the markings of some alien and antique serpent, rare and beautiful and lethal, and the wood was figured with a deep red feather grain at the butt and held a small springloaded silver capbox in the toe. (BM 265–66)

But the gun's fate mirrors the outcome of every effort to establish order in *Blood Meridian*. Caring nothing about the shotgun's workmanship, Brown saws off its barrels to make an even more destructive weapon. Everything and everybody — individuals, families, towns — fall before the rampaging scalp hunters.

There appears, moreover, little hope for religious salvation amidst all the destruction, despite the numerous biblical references that dot the novel. But these dots never connect, never coalesce into a pattern either for understanding the bleak and incomprehensible void or for transcending it. The powerlessness of religious faith is signaled not only by the overwhelming power of the scalp hunters in their marauding — made immediately clear in the opening pages when the Judge turns a tent revival into a riot — but also by McCarthy's narrative stance. As Dana Phillips observes, McCarthy writes with an "optical democracy," a perspective that foregrounds the immense history of the natural world. From this long view, the human is not privileged over the nonhuman — all existence stands equally in the same continuum. Matters of the spirit have little, if any significance, in this vast continuum. "Salvation history, which understands the natural world and man's travails in it as symbols of the spirit, has long been played out, as the ruined, eroded, and buzzard-draped mission churches in *Blood Meridian* suggest," Phillips writes. "Only natural history, which regards neither nature nor man as symbolic, is left." [18] Phillips goes on to argue that McCarthy's paradigm of natural history presents the contemporary world "as an ancient world not of myth but of rock and stone and those life forms that can endure the daily cataclysms of heat and cold and hunger, that can weather the everyday round of random, chaotic violence." McCarthy, Phillips concludes, "is not a writer of the 'modern' or 'postmodern' eras, but of the Holocene." [19] The repeated descriptions of Glanton's men disappearing into the landscape manifest on a smaller scale the narrative's occlusion of human significance.

In scattering human existence into the vastness of geologic time, McCarthy's far-reaching perspective — one that takes a Southern interest in the historical imagination to its limits, to the beginning of time — underscores the flimsiness of culturally constructed borders and boundaries, particularly those fundamental to a culture's understanding of itself, those separating civilized and uncivilized, human and animal, reason and madness, and so on. Rather than resting upon and establishing essential truth, these borders merely validate humanity's puny impositions upon a finally untamable and unfathomable world, a point underscored in *Blood Meridian*'s epilogue.

The epilogue describes a man punching a line of postholes into a prairie littered with bones, his effort described as "less the pursuit of some continuance than the verification of a principle, a validation of sequence and causality as if each round and perfect hole owed its existence to the one before it there on that prairie upon which are the bones and the gatherers of bones and those who do not gather" (BM 337). The hole digger's faith in sequence and causality is indeed just that—faith, not order itself. His effort to line the plain calls to mind the project of the federal government to divide up the vacant lands west of the Mississippi in perfect grids of one hundred and sixty acres each for homesteading, with no regard for the lay of the land — or anything else, for that matter. The government's plan embodies the Enlightenment dream of perfect order, a world in which nature and society are ordered with geometric precision and beauty. This foolhardy graphing of the natural world, an action perhaps as crucial to the opening of the West as the savage Indian wars described in the rest of *Blood Meridian*, leads in McCarthy's eyes not to an agrarian paradise but to the killing fields — prairies littered with the bones that the posthole digger ignores as he works to lay down his straight line. This line across the prairie is McCarthy's line of Western history, his blood meridian, a line following the dream of progress, a line pursuing order and empire that leads straight to chaos and mayhem.

By the time of McCarthy's Border Trilogy—*All the Pretty Horses* (1992), *The Crossing* (1994), and *Cities of the Plain* (1998)—the West is latticed with lines: roads, fences, telephone lines, power lines. Divided and subdivided, McCarthy's West of the mid–twentieth century is filling up not only with ranches and towns but also, even more significantly, with military bases. These outposts of progress represent the end point of McCarthy's blood meridian — the military-industrial complex. Indeed, from the killing fields of the nineteenth century, we move to the killing fields of the twentieth; the Enlightenment dream of plotting out the world has led in the twentieth century to the splitting of the atom, the most efficient weapon of all. If McCarthy is the writer of the Holocene in *Blood Meridian,* he is the writer of the apocalypse in the Border Trilogy: overhanging the three novels is not only the threat to traditional life posed by the ever-expanding military-industrial complex and technological society but also the threat of nuclear annihilation.[20]

The threat posed by the military grows progressively as the trilogy proceeds. World War II looms as the backdrop to the action, particularly the tremendous changes the war and the home front war effort render to the West, from the loss of men in battle overseas to the re-making of the land and the social order at home in the creation of military bases, research centers, testing grounds, and extensive supply and support systems. John Grady Cole's father introduces the military theme early in *All the Pretty Horses* when he tells his son that, years earlier, his going off to war contributed to the dissolution of his marriage. It was not merely his going away that hurt the marriage; it was the fact that soldiering changed him in some fundamental way. "It aint her fault," he says, speaking of his wife, "I aint the same as I was. I'd like to think I am. But I aint."[21] John Grady's father also notes that the way of life in the West was somehow fundamentally changed, though he cannot quite figure out how. The West will never be the same again, he says, adding that "people dont feel safe no more. . . . We're like the Commanches was two hundred years ago. We dont know what's goin to show up here come daylight. We dont even know what color they'll be" (APH 25–26). John Grady's father clearly feels that a larger power now controls the West, and though he does not specifically name that power, he suggests its military origins in his reference to the Commanches and the fear of cavalry raids — an echo of the world of *Blood Meridian,* with the military-industrial complex as a modern-day manifestation of the scalp hunters and with ordinary citizens entirely at the system's mercy.

The enigmatic and elusive comments in *All the Pretty Horses* about the military and the changing West become much more specific and grounded in *The Crossing*, which is set during World War II, a few years earlier than the previous novel takes place. In his wanderings throughout Mexico, Billy Parham is entirely ignorant of the war, but on his return to the United States on his second trip, he immediately learns of the conflict and sees how it is remaking the land he had left. When he speaks to the border guard as he crosses into New Mexico, he tells him that he hopes to join up with an outfit. Billy is speaking of becoming a ranch hand, but the guard misunderstands, thinking he wants to enlist as a soldier. The miscommunication speaks volumes about the remade West, the cowboy transformed into soldier: "outfit," besides suggesting the new military order, also suggests the new garb of the West—the military uniform. Once the proving ground for the American hero, the West, now militarized, has become the proving ground for missiles and bombs. Hawks have become Hawk missiles; Indian reservations, military reservations; open ranges, firing ranges. The vocabulary of the mythic West has been appropriated for purposes of the military-industrial state.

Billy is utterly lost in this new world. He has no home and no destination; as he explains to an army doctor regarding the fact that he was from Cloverdale, "I was but I aint no more. I dont have anyplace to go." [22] Billy tries to enlist in the army, and thus to enter into the new order of the West, but when he is rejected because of a heart defect, he begins a life of wandering, trying to eke out an existence by working anywhere he can. Uncertainty rules his—and everyone else's—life. "This war," an old rancher tells him. "There's no way to calculate what's to come" (C 345). Not long after hearing this, Billy thinks about the new world in which he finds himself, commenting that "the one thing he knew of all things claimed to be known was that there was no certainty to any of it. Not just the coming of war. Anything at all" (346).

The Crossing ends with the twentieth century's most frightening image of uncertainty and anxiety, the atomic blast. Adrift and about to set off on further wanderings, Billy awakens before sunrise to witness an atomic dawn, with sky glowing and wind whipping up from a nuclear explosion—certainly the test blast that took place at the "Trinity Site" at 5:29 A.M. on 16 July 1945. The Trinity test is the new morning of McCarthy's trilogy, the ushering in of a new age—the nuclear age—dominated by the military-industrial complex and the threat of nuclear annihilation. It is an age marked by the disruption of the natural order—the splitting of the atom, matter's fundamental unit—a disorder signaled here in Billy's waking to two dawns. As a historian of the Trinity test put it, the day of that explosion was the day when "the sun rose twice."[23] In the crushing final sentences of *The Crossing,* Billy sits before the approaching second dawn and weeps, not only for all that he has lost but for what is to come in this rapidly changing world: "He took off his hat and placed it on the tarmac before him and he bowed his head and held his face in his hands and wept. He sat there for a long time and after a while the east did gray and after a while the right and godmade sun did rise, once again, for all and without distinction" (C 426).

By the time of *Cities of the Plain*—the early 1950s, when nuclear testing is proceeding at ferocious levels—the military-industrial complex appears on the verge of completely engulfing the West and its way of life. The air force base in Alamogordo, New Mexico, is now threatening, as part of the government's expansion of missile testing, to annex the ranch on which John Grady and Billy work.[24] A curtain of doom and uncertainty hangs everywhere; it is clear that the old ways of life, the cowboy life, are coming to an end, and it is not clear what the future holds. At one point John Grady and Billy ponder what they would do if they were not cowboys. They cannot think of anything. They talk about starting over in Mexico, but they know it is a pipe dream. There is no place for them anymore.

Indeed, John Grady and Billy inhabit a dwindling space lodged between the Alamogordo military base and the Mexican border, the former representing the inevitable future and the latter the romantic dream of Western independence and freedom. Throughout most of McCarthy's Border Trilogy, Mexico stands as a land of mystery and adventure — it is the legendary West for John Grady and Billy, a land of unchecked freedom and possibility. But by the time of *Cities of the Plain*, Mexico has become for the boys merely Mexico-as-border-town, a place to go for liquor and prostitutes. Although characters in *Cities* still speak of Mexico as an alien and mysterious land, it is actually only about as strange as any red-light district. *Cities* opens in a brothel with John Grady, Billy, and a friend dickering over the choice of women — that's what adventure in Mexico has now become.

Cities of the Plain carries to fruition the destruction of the traditional West — its land and way of life overrun by forces of modernity — that began in the previous two novels. The novel ends quietly, jumping ahead fifty years to just after the millennium, with Billy now an old man and adrift. At the novel's close, he is taken in and given succor by a woman to whose home he has wandered. The woman's grace and charity, which conclude the novel and the trilogy, suggest that in a world come so undone, so lost to the forces of science and modernity, simple gestures of kindness and good will are humanity's most genuine and heroic acts. Those characters throughout the Border Trilogy who act selflessly in helping others — the workers who stop for the wounded Boyd and the doctor who treats him; the judge who counsels John Grady after his return from Mexico; the unnamed families in Mexico who offer food and shelter to John Grady and Billy merely because they are travelers—are finally McCarthy's heroes, those who know that bonds of humanity and fellowship are all we have to help us along in the ever-darkening world. The comforting power of these bonds is underscored in the message McCarthy sends us away with in *Cities*'s epilogue:

DEDICATION

I will be your child to hold
And you be me when I am old
The world grows cold
The heathen rage
The story's told
Turn the page.

It is a stunningly domestic conclusion (hinting both of the enduring power of the human spirit and also of Christian salvation) to McCarthy's stunningly undomestic trilogy, which chronicles the destruction of the West by forces of twentieth-century "civilization" and "progress."

In ways similar to Dickey's and McCarthy's, Madison Smartt Bell's *Zero db and Other Stories* (1987) interrogates notions of civilization and progress through the manipulation of the Western. As do Dickey's and McCarthy's, Bell's fiction characteristically strips away the constructions of culture to portray the elemental, foregrounding borders and border crossings, particularly those between humanity and the natural world. But whereas Dickey and McCarthy focus most intently on the violent underpinnings of culture that are masked by the ideology of America's manifest destiny, Bell levels his gaze primarily on the spiritual emptiness of that destiny. Unlike Dickey's and McCarthy's portrayals of a lurking bestiality at the heart of humanity, Bell portrays a lurking divinity, a spirituality that links humanity with the universe but that has been suppressed by the materialism of modern culture. "Today Is a Good Day to Die," the Western tale that closes *Zero db*, explores this repression of the spirit and, in terms of its place in the collection, lays the groundwork for and illuminates all the spiritual quests undertaken in the other stories.

Zero db is remarkably diverse, peopled with quirky characters from the rural South and the urban North struggling to make their lives substantial. They seek fundamental, down-to-earth experiences, hoping to break out of their everyday routines in order to live more vitally. An admirer of Walker Percy, Bell shares Percy's concern that most people in today's society see only what society has conditioned them to see.[25] People experience wonder and delight not by observing the world's mysterious nature but rather by measuring how well what they observe matches up to their preformed expectations. The thing itself, in all its mystery, is lost.

Recovering the mystery of creation is what most of Bell's characters seek, primarily by being close observers of the world. Looking and listening at things long and hard enough can shatter the preformed symbolic complex, the way a word becomes meaningless sound when endlessly repeated. "Listen. Listen. Listen," says the narrator of the story "Zero db." "We can never be too attentive to our world."[26] Another close observer, the narrator of "Dormitory and Food Services," finds great joy — and apparently, great meaning — by staring at a brick wall outside his window and listening to cars passing: "The acoustics of the alley simultaneously cushioned and amplified the noise of the cars that swished up and down the street, thus creating a very soothing and restful sound for me to listen to. And the opposite wall was really lovely in its own way. Its bricks were all the different brick colors, and some of them were blue, and they altered their shades as the time of day changed. I could have watched them forever, and in fact I almost did" (ZDB 67). Experiencing things by surprise, particularly in situations out of everyday context, can also dismantle the preformed complex, as happens when a young girl in "Triptych I" sees the strands of blood from a dead hog trailing down through the creek. The complicated patterns of the strands bring her to ponder the nature of blood, to imagine blood *as* blood, to dream about how blood carries life as it courses through the body. She is completely lost to her vision of blood's mysteries, her eyes "clear and empty as the sky" (ZDB 20).

Emptying one's eyes — clearing the preformed symbolic complexes from them — suggests a stripping-away motion crucial to almost all of Bell's stories. Characters repeatedly divest themselves of everything but the bare-bone essentials for survival. They give away possessions, they withdraw into solitary rooms and routines, they sit around doing little but observing and listening. The narrator of "Irene," for instance, spends almost all his time observing the people and objects in his urban neighborhood; the narrator of "Zero db" believes that his "greatest hope and ambition might be to emulate this beautiful machine [his tape recorder]. Or that I need no other reason for being other than to contemplate it" (ZDB 148). The most difficult problem for Bell's questers — modern-day versions of the Desert Fathers who retreated to the desert seeking spiritual vision through rigid ascetic practice — is the crushing boredom they face. Try as they might to hold it off, the everyday inevitably comes crashing back; solitary contemplation becomes the mundane. "There came a day when nothing that I saw seemed new," the narrator of "Irene" says, adding that "it's theoretically true that boredom comes from a dulling of your own perceptions and not from any diminution of the world outside. But boredom is boring nonetheless" (ZDB 78–79). A number of stories from *Zero db* are told retrospectively, with characters wistfully recalling former days when they felt more alive and vital and when they were still seeking the wondrous. In the end, almost all of Bell's characters fall prey to the grinding forces of necessity, practicality, and conformity.

This is the contemporary world that Bell uses to ground *Zero db*'s final story, "Today Is a Good Day to Die," a Western set in the late nineteenth century during the campaign against the Plains Indians. As jarring as it seems at first glance in the overall context of the collection, "Today Is a Good Day to Die" is crucial to *Zero db*'s narrative and thematic structure, contextualizing all the more quirky and less dramatic quests that come earlier in the text but later in chronological time. It is the story of a young army lieutenant during his posting to the Western territories in 1875 and 1876. The lieutenant has come west by his own choosing, desiring both to help further America's manifest destiny and to escape the genteel culture of the East. Before long, however, he develops into another of Bell's spiritual questers and begins a process of withdrawal, both from his friends and family back in the East (he finds it harder and harder to write letters home and eventually gives up) and from those about him. He is most happy when on solitary rides into the snow-covered wastes, described as a perfect blankness where "there is no date, no time" (ZDB 164).

A crucial encounter occurs during one of the lieutenant's rides. Lost and close to succumbing to the cold, he meets two Indians, one of whom revives him after he lapses into unconsciousness. Although they can communicate only with images etched in the snow, the lieutenant recognizes in the Indian's "deep stillness" a profound and inexpressible knowledge. As he sits with his rescuer, the lieutenant feels "words jounce against one another in his mind until all their expressiveness is worn away"; he "is alive with questions he cannot formulate. . . . what he wants to know he cannot even phrase in English" (ZDB 169). Initially attempting to merge his civilized knowledge with that of the Indian (following the classic pattern of the frontier hero as discussed by Fiedler and Slotkin), the lieutenant soon begins a process going one step further: he attempts to shed entirely his white identity to embrace that of the Indian. Back at the fort, he retreats further into himself, coming to regard soldiering as pointless and seeing America's manifest destiny in the opening up of the West as "a long trajectory to nowhere" (171).

Ultimately, the lieutenant abandons the army, walking away from the aftermath of the Battle of the Little Big Horn in order to follow "the Indian practice of seeking guidance by going alone into the desert to dream" (172). Following the trail of the Indian fighters, and no longer the line of American destiny, he progressively discards his possessions, seeking, like Bell's other questers, to empty himself of the material so as to be filled with the spiritual. After three days without food and water, the lieutenant finally collapses and receives his vision: "He sees a wraithlike shape, not soul but a dark devouring shadow, rise out of his suppurating body and march inexorably over the mountains to the sea. The lieutenant is happy that this thing has left him, and relieved that its future will never be his own." Now happily emptied of the compulsive desire to push west, the lieutenant settles into and embraces his place in the natural world, a brotherhood of all living things. The story closes with the first of many awaiting buzzards lighting next to him. *"Brother, I greet you,"* the lieutenant says; *"Take and eat what God hath given thee"* (ZDB 179).

No doubt mad by society's standards, the lieutenant in his "madness" interrogates those very standards.[27] His search brings to light the destructive impulses embedded in American expansionism and, more generally, in the capitalist ideologies of the modern industrial state—we know from the other stories in *Zero db* where America is headed in the late twentieth century. Moreover, his quest for the world's divinity points to the fact that spirituality has been overwhelmed by the materialism of the modern world. To seek this divinity calls for the radical divestiture of modernity, precisely what the lieutenant attempts, in a move that recalls Bell's other questers, those madcap ascetics in contemporary America who look for mystery in brick walls and dead hogs. If the lieutenant literally plunges west, retreating to the desert rather than returning to society, Bell's other questers head metaphorically west, plunging themselves into the desert of the modern condition.

Zero db finally suggests that in postmodern America the West and the Western legend have little to do with geography. The West—the desert, emptied of culture—can be found anywhere; discovering fundamental experience is a matter of vision, of sight and insight, of emptying one's eyes, of cleansing oneself of material desires. Or, as Michael L. Johnson puts it in *New Westers*, the West is "as much a mental as a geographical landscape. . . . a kind of 'virtual reality'— and thus, to an extent, virtual meaning, virtual heritage, virtual values."[28] Seeking the West means leaving the everyday world behind, even if one does not move an inch; it means pushing beyond the cultural, but not necessarily the geographic, borders of civilization, stepping free from the fundamental ideologies of society and into the wilderness of unmediated confrontation with the here and now. In striving to push beyond cultural frontiers, Bell's questers in the end drift toward becoming the alien others against which society defines itself, as with the lieutenant who strives to become an Indian, a person who must be displaced and destroyed for modernity's advance.

Heading west for Bell thus finally means heading toward literal death but spiritual wholeness — and thus the lieutenant's greeting to the vultures. Approaching death, he is now moving toward participating in the divine order of the universe; it is, then, certainly a good day to die.[29] In a culture of materialism and consumption — the modern world as Bell depicts it throughout *Zero db* — no day ever is a good day to die, since the material, the body, is all people have. The lieutenant's joyful acceptance of death calls that materialism into question, pointing the way toward Bell's stunning affirmation of a spirituality lost to the modern condition.

If the lieutenant's quest in "Today Is a Good Day to Die" illuminates those of Bell's other questers, the corporatism and materialism of contemporary American culture in these other stories from *Zero db* shed light on America's push west, which the lieutenant at first endorses and then flees from. Bell suggests a connection that the Nashville Agrarians years earlier argued explicitly: the origins of American capitalism lie in the aggressive pioneering spirit that has shaped our national history and mythology. It is that history and mythology from which the lieutenant — and Bell's other questers — seeks refuge, searching for spaces alive with rather than dead to the spirit.

What looms as the backdrop of Bell's "Today Is a Good Day to Die" becomes the foreground of Barry Hannah's *Never Die* (1991), a novel that explodes the myth of Western innocence and pioneer heroism by portraying Western enterprise as just that — enterprise, cold-hearted pursuit of power and money. Hannah, of course, is no stranger to the debunking of myths, though usually he sets his sights on those permeating his native Dixie, particularly those lies (as he likes to call them) involving masculinity, honor, and heroism. As Ruth Weston has observed, much of Hannah's fiction centers on the trope of lying, with Hannah's heroes piercingly aware that cultural myths are entirely socially constructed, rather than expressions of universal truths, and yet lovingly embracing them anyway. In manifesting this dual awareness, Hannah's fiction thus simultaneously celebrates *and* debunks cultural myths; for Hannah, it is far better to aspire with joy to an ideal, even if that ideal is completely insubstantial, than it is to wallow in despair and inaction. Weston comments on Hannah's vision and his characters' struggles with the myths of manhood: "Hannah writes about the American male's individual and lonely search for an absolute dream of manly behavior among cultural memories and expectations that continually betray him. The narrative rhythm achieved by his characters' vacillating preoccupations with the dream, the cultural lie, and their obsessive need to confess their complicity in the process constitutes a 'metronome ticking' throughout 'the whole lying opera' of Hannah's fiction."[30]

There is certainly a great deal of debunking of cultural legends in Hannah's Western, *Never Die*, particularly of the West as a space for regenerative and heroic endeavor. Reverend McCorkindale's characterization of the West as "drunken eruption and hangover" points to the fact that for most people in Hannah's West life indeed is something close to a hangover—tedious, paltry, boring.[31] Fernando's forced idleness, because of his kneecapping by Smoot, speaks for almost all of the people in Nitburg, themselves crippled, psychologically if not literally. "Out West, you got all the time in the world to practice" (ND 55), Fernando tells Nermer after he has knocked him down and drawn his gun with blazing speed. This is not a timeless world but a time-saturated world, not unlike that sleepy Southern town about which Robert Penn Warren wrote; there is too much time, with so little to do that the hours and days seem endless and oppressive.

Most everyone in *Never Die* is bored almost to senselessness. Sheriff Neb Lewton's inaction—he is described as being "with cobwebs between his thumb and trigger finger, rust flaking out of his rectum" (ND 4)—typifies the idleness pervading Hannah's West. Those who, like Fernando, ponder their inaction generally end up wallowing in self-pity, despair, and cynicism, driving themselves ever deeper into numbing depression and stasis. "The bitterness is wearing me down, making me frown in my sleep, making my tits wilt and things of that nature," Fernando thinks at one point. "He was so sad he was turning androgynous" (7), observes the narrator, who later describes Fernando's misery: "Sad, sad, he was deeply sad. He had forgotten what sadness intense physical pain brought on. What could he accomplish? Alone, he screamed out, 'You think I can stand this? Thrown in here with my pointless mental life? God damn it'" (21–22). Eventually Fernando does pull himself up from his despair to act, but it is only because of the extremity of the situations he faces and because he is Fernando, the hero.

If Fernando finally gets moving because of his desire to do good, most of the other people in Hannah's West, when they're not idle, are acting merely out of lust or greed. "Guess that's about all there is," Luther Nix says. "Money and sex. And grit" (ND 115). There are countless numbers of sexual pursuits—and assaults—in *Never Die*, and there are just as many efforts to make money. Everyone seems to have a money-making scheme, even Fernando, who dreams of opening a coffin factory. Rather than being wiped clean of civilization, Hannah's West is smeared with it; Nitburg is not a new world but merely the old world transplanted into the new. It is American society at its most fundamental — unadorned acquisitiveness. Hannah's West is thus less a wilderness where people pursue regeneration through ordeal and violence than a world to be made into a prosperous, money-making system. Nitburg is a plantation without the cotton fields, a factory town without the factory. It is pure capitalist enterprise, with Judge Nitburg as the boss.

But Nitburg is more than boss — he is creator. He came to the West to found his town precisely because nothing was there yet. Before he moved out to the region, he gazed longingly over a map, tracing the line of the Colorado River — a scene reminiscent of the opening of *Deliverance* and perhaps a reference to Conrad's *Heart of Darkness*. In searching out a place to create his empire, Nitburg zeroed in on a dot that was a faraway hamlet, a place "even the map seemed barely interested in" (ND 92). He fell into an ecstatic rapture, dreaming of his future success: "While he was at the map, he touched himself and exuded a pleasant sweat. Here was real creation. Here was enterprise" (93). We know the lengths to which Nitburg as capitalist will pursue lucre. Before he founds his town, Nitburg has already received one hundred dollars for turning his mother in as a Confederate spy (he then watched her execution), sold a wife to the Indians for four thousand dollars in gold, married a blind millionaire widow seventeen years his senior ("Who was the fool who prescribed passion for marriage, with its drool and jealousies?" he asks [91]), and run a tenement complex, collecting rent and selling supplies (mostly alcohol and drugs) through his store, creating a perfect money-making machine in which "a happy rotation of the dead and mad [are] hauled off by healthier alcoholics who worked for him" (91). Orphans he sold to goldrushers.

All of these enterprises, however, pale in scope before his creation of the town that bears his name. If even Nitburg at times recognizes the questionable ethics of his previous dealings — "all his lies and secrecy behind him like the diarrhea of a millionaire" (ND 30) — he has no qualms about what he does in running his town. As creator, as the bringer of civilization, he proclaims: "The effect of my life, this struggle on the darkling plain, has been creation, quite from practically nothing, I might add. Men, like me or not, you are staring at civilization. Fate has prepared me, and I am a special kind. When there was nothing and then there is something, whatever that is, is right. When there is nothing to eat and then there is something to eat, that is good. Gentlemen, I am the last water in the well. Not so tasty, perhaps, but water, and it is right" (ND 96). Nitburg needs no justification. He created the system and the system justifies itself: quite simply, power is the foundation and the organizing principle of cultural order.

Opposed to Nitburg is Fernando, the gunslinger hero who wants to burn the town down and cleanse it of its evil. Fernando, however, is anything but the man in the white hat, the unstained and upstanding hero of classic Westerns who alone does battle with forces of evil. Like everyone else, he has dreams of riches; he is a drunkard; he has stolen mail from Wells Fargo; he has served time in prison. But even more significantly he is a man of inaction — "a creature of perfect idleness" (ND 5), "a born idler" (23). "Ennui be my middle name," Fernando says, "but I moves it from place to place" (25). His only claim to fame as a hero is that he once killed three men in a gunfight. That episode was anything but heroic, however, with Fernando crouching behind an overturned poker table — grasping his groin with one hand and his gun with the other — firing blindly at his attackers. He was, as the narrator writes, "a gunfighter almost without intending to be" (3).

Fernando, in other words, is less a hero because of what he is or has done than because people desperately want to believe in heroes and the heroic. For this reason, the townspeople configure Fernando as glorious and vital, the gunslinger hero of the legendary West, despite the fact that he is as lazy and shiftless as everyone else. "Fernando, how I admire that man," says Neb Newton. "God give him a few talents and he didn't hide them under a bushel like me, not at all. He went after it. The rest of us just shuffle and wait, and before you know it, what, shit, natural causes, another dumb casualty, with so much promise" (ND 118). But such lionization is all a lie, and Fernando more than anyone knows that his heroic image is as fictional as the legendary West. "Comes to the point where you ain't nothing but a couple of stories blowing around like a weed," he tells Stella; "You can't even keep none of your promises. And you're not even none of those stories anymore" (83).

Eventually, of course, Fernando becomes a hero, living up to the stories about him, as he burns down a large chunk of Nitburg and defeats the Judge's hired killers. "A man has to stand up and do," he tells Stella (ND 84), and that's exactly what he does. But after the terrific shoot-out, Fernando retreats to his uncle's ranch, "a burned-scarred half-crippled recluse" (150), spurning the heroic role that people now bestow even more enthusiastically upon him. Despite his withdrawal, and probably in part because of it, his admirers only further inflate his image. "Every day, more light from behind, more softness, more gauze," Philip Hine says to Nermer and then later to Fernando. "It's time we held the dance of history. You're all heroes, and folks will miss your kind. History won't let you hate yourselves anymore" (152). Fernando knows better, and he tells Hine that he is wrong, that he is no hero, but he adds that he does now have plans to act for the good and that he figures he has a better chance this time around of acting well. As an aging, broken-down man, he has no lies to live up to other than those of his own making; he can do well in small ways, and they are ways that matter to him and to those about whom he cares.

Fernando's words to Hine, which close the novel, both debunk and celebrate heroic ideals, a double motion characteristic of Hannah's imaginative sensibility and the narrative pattern of *Never Die*. As underscored in this final conversation, together with the novel's title, the cultural lie of heroic endeavor — that heroes never die but live forever in legendary narratives — glosses over the fact that people do indeed live, suffer, and die and that heroes rarely live up to the stories told about them. Fernando embraces a true heroism at the end, deciding to do good for its own sake; by repudiating the heroic, he becomes the hero, turning his back on the world of gritty enterprise that is Hannah's West. Fernando no longer looks the part of the Western hero, lacking the swagger and the clothes, but those things, as Fernando signals with his knowing smile to Hine, are merely adornments of the great lie of the West in which he is no longer participating.

Like Hannah's *Never Die*, Clyde Edgerton's *Redeye* (1995) explores the great lie of American expansion, presenting the West less as a place of legendary heroes than of cultural mythmaking — and moneymaking. Indeed, the novel's narrative frame — a 1905 expedition guidebook — not only reveals the lies of the Western legend (the story it presents and comments on everywhere fails to live up to its billing) but also shows how the Western legend has largely been shaped by an enterprising tourist industry. Come to the Wild West, the title page of the guidebook proclaims; it is "a trip you will NEVER FORGET!" There you will find "TRUE STORIES OF WILD WEST ADVENTURE / DEPICTIONS OF MEN OF BOTH NOBLE & QUESTIONABLE CHARACTER / TALES OF WILD DOGS & SAVAGE INDIANS." This is the West as spectacle — not stunning landscape but flamboyant commodification. It is the selling of the West, the West of tourism and souvenirs. As the guidebook announces, the real West is long gone, accessible now only through "Wild West" reenactments—precisely what the guidebook itself promotes.

In its packaging of the Wild West as tourist spectacle, the guidebook presents its version of Western settlement, what it declares is an epic story of civilization's advance. The guidebook's author, William Blankenship, himself one of region's most enterprising moneymakers, proclaims that capitalist entrepreneurs are the heroes of this march of progress. Early on, the guidebook identifies Blankenship as a "community leader and developer of the scenic, natural, cultural, anthropological, and touristic resources of Mumford Rock and her region," adding that he and Copeland (along with the railroads) "figured in the modernization of the West in the latter part of the last century through their contributions to the 'civil' in civilization. Without Blankenship's leadership surely our territory would 'lag' in the march out of the old century into the new." [32] In this gilded version of the capitalism's exploitation of people and nature, the spirit of entrepreneurship—of making a buck—represents not only wisdom and foresight but also philanthropy. After noting that "there existed in the expanding, progressive little town of Mumford Rock, Colorado, that spirit of experimentation that would characterize all of America in those years," the guidebook praises the increasing pace of modern inventions, pointing to "the steam engine, the cotton gin, the telephone, and other advancements representing a true philanthropic spirit" (R 160).

Of course, the story of Mumford Rock's development—and particularly Blankenship's shenanigans in the enterprise—is anything but philanthropic, let alone wise. In the passages immediately following the guidebook's discussion of modern inventions and philanthropy,

Blankenship organizes an experiment to run electricity through an Indian mummy in hopes of reviving her—she would be a much better tourist attraction if she could talk. Elsewhere he compares his far-sighted spirit of experimentation with that of Isaac Newton, but the experiments of this self-proclaimed Newton are self-serving rather than scientific—they include blowing up a corpse with dynamite to promote his embalming business by illustrating what can happen to bodies not embalmed and devising a plan to put Grandma Copeland in a display box posing as a revived mummy. When her son, P. J., objects, saying "that's my *mama* you're talking about," Blankenship responds, "I know that, P. J. I know that. But I'm also talking about *business*. I'm also talking about capital. I'm also talking about money. I'm also talking about what tourists is going to do for your saddle trade. I'm also talking what those two fine coffins on display will do to Modern Mortuary Science Services, Incorporated. In short, I'm talking about *life*" (R 202). He adds a bit later: "In the coming few years half the world is going to get rich entertaining the other half, which is going to be poor. I want to be in that first half" (203). Here's the true philanthropic spirit of capitalism's development of the West.

Redeye ends with an advertisement proclaiming "RUPTURE PERMANENTLY CURED OR NO PAY." Seeming at first glance to be merely one more example of Edgerton's delight in playing with frontier humor, the advertisement underscores the rupture between the high-flown rhetoric of the guidebook, which gives the "authorized" version of the West's history, and the mundane, if not at times sordid, goings-on in the stories within. As hard as the guidebook strives to mask the West's history of exploitation and enterprise in the spectacle of the "Wild West," the stories it tells are too disruptive for its palliative to work. As do the other Southern writers who write Westerns, Edgerton explores the rupture of the seemingly secure cultural boundaries established by the American mythology of the West. For him and the other writers, these cultural boundaries are not really boundaries at all, only wished-for and violently imposed dreams of empire, and dreams that disappear into thin air when one looks closely at the violence — economic, military, and racial — that lies at the heart of, and is masked by, the frontier legend.

Rupture in *Redeye* also characterizes the frontier experiences of Edgerton's characters and in this regard looks forward to the work of Southerners who write about the contemporary West. Star, for instance, a Southern woman who moves to the West, sheds the frills of refined culture and is transformed by her Western experiences. For the strong-willed folk like Star who head west, rupture means breaking free from constraint, a move ultimately leading to growth and fulfillment. As we will see in the next chapter, many of the Southern writers who write about the contemporary West explore this type of rupture — a stepping free from everyday life and routine that propels people westward in search of individual freedom. But ultimately it is a rupture, as the final advertisement in *Redeye* suggests, that does indeed need healing. Although it is never made explicit, Star may have found too much freedom in the West; at the end of the novel, she has left the West and is back in North Carolina, an independent woman working as an advocate for women's higher education. Southern writers writing about the contemporary West will follow Star's lead, looking for ways to heal the rupture between freedom and confinement, between the impulses to fly west into space and to stay home and create a life in place.

3 / Regeneration through Community

Recent Southern writers who write about the contemporary West represent a wide cross section of Southern fiction. Despite their diverse styles and interests, almost all of these authors utilize and revise the American myth of flight westward toward freedom. Driving the narrative in almost all of their work is the dream of stepping free from the confining nets of culture and of starting over with the past left tidily behind. Almost all of these works, in the end, make it clear that this dream is indeed just that—a dream, and one that taken to its extreme becomes a nightmare, calling to mind Bernard DeVoto's observation, as restated by Wallace Stegner, "that the only true individualists in the West had wound up on one end of a rope whose other end was in the hands of a bunch of cooperators." [1] A number of the works explicitly explore the terrifying manifestations that the quest for radical freedom can take, such as that in Chris Offutt's *The Good Brother*, where a man in flight gets involved with a group of armed-to-the-teeth survivalists. Even when the lesson is not so dramatic, the message in these works remains clear: the desire for radical individual freedom leads down dangerous and self-destructive paths. For all their apparent turning from the traditional Southern ideals of place and continuity, Southerners writing about the contemporary West in the end embrace something very close to those very ideals, even if the place where their characters finally settle is often far from Dixie.

Structuring almost all of these works is a tension between the desire to bolt for freedom, a centrifugal force flying outward, and the desire to settle in a community, a centripetal force pulling inward. If most of these works begin with a straight line heading west, the tension between these two forces characteristically pulls that line back into a circle, the two forces now taut and balanced around a center point of home and community. The completed circle represents not enclosure but balance — balance between freedom and responsibility, conscience and selfishness, remembering and forgetting. And so, as much as these works center on flight and escape, they end up being most fundamentally about settling in and establishing communities. Not that the flights westward are meaningless; they are almost always necessary for breaking away from rigid and confining lives, but in almost every case they are finally abandoned for a life in place, not space.

The first contemporary Southern novel about bolting westward, Doris Betts's appropriately titled *Heading West* (1983), follows this pattern closely, as does her more recent novel, *The Sharp Teeth of Love* (1997). The female protagonists of these novels, Nancy and Luna, flee to the West to escape the confinement of damaging domesticity. As Nancy declares, heading west is her "declaration of independence," her manifest destiny.[2] Both women, however, after taking charge of themselves and their destinies in the stark Western landscape, end up swinging back toward domesticity. They now know the limits of both unchecked freedom and domestic enslavement, and they now seek something in between: nurturing rather than oppressive home lives, lives of individual freedom and commitment within relationships. Domesticity itself is not the villain here; rather, it is a particular sort of domesticity, one that locks women into subservience and domestic martyrdom so that they are always serving others, never themselves. It is a domestic model distinctly, though of course not uniquely, Southern, a modern-day version of the Southern belle, minus the hoop skirts and stays.

Nancy's flight to the West in *Heading West* begins as anything but a bolt toward freedom: she is kidnapped by a young crook named Dwight, who carries her along on his drive west. What begins as a terrifying ordeal quickly becomes Nancy's means of personal liberation. Before her abduction, she has lived a tepid life as an unmarried small-town librarian, devoting herself to taking care of her quirky and demanding family. She cannot bring herself to cut loose, much as she desperately wants to. Her kidnapping, paradoxically, brings her escape, with Dwight forcibly ripping her away from her stultifying life back home. After a few rough and scary moments with Dwight, Nancy becomes so enthused about the drive west that she not only does not try to escape but goes out of her way to keep Dwight from getting caught — she even slips away to go to a pharmacy to get birth control pills just in case something happens between her and Dwight. She does not want the trip to end because she does not want to go home. She wants to keep heading west.

Nancy's enthusiasm in her flight lies not merely in being free from her family — it is even more liberating to be free from her conscience, from her compulsion to take care of others. When a friend asks her later why she did not run from Dwight, Nancy responds that "all that time I *was* running, but running away from home" and that there was something enjoyable about having matters taken out of her hands, about "taking a vacation from conscience" (HW 297). It is precisely this freedom from conscience that Nancy finds so intriguing in Dwight. "Dwight did exactly what he wanted and if he was never satisfied, he was never guilty, either," she observes after her ordeal. "It was fascinating. What makes some people turn out that way and some others become such nasty martyrs?" (302).

Nancy does eventually flee from Dwight, not because she wants to return home (she does not) but because she wants to forge ahead west on her own, without him and the other rider, Judge Jolley, who has joined them on their trip. She comes to see the situation in the car developing into one similar to that at home, with Nancy as the administering angel, taking care of everyone's needs. She wants none of that now, and so she bolts, to pursue a new life completely free of her past and other people. As she thinks at one point, heading west on her own is her means of achieving personal happiness. Her happiness. Nobody else's. She imagines her new life beginning with her happily forgetting who she is and where she is from. "Nancy yearned toward that amnesia," the narrator tells us, and Nancy herself fantasizes, "I'll be a woman from Sandia Pueblo with no relatives. Speaking in Tigua. I can start over with a clear conscience" (HW 115–16).

Nancy gets just what she wants, or almost. After her showdown in the Grand Canyon with Dwight and her later collapse from heat prostration, she wakes up in the hospital with no identification and with nobody around who knows who she is. It is the perfect opportunity for her new beginning, her past wiped completely clean, and at first she embraces it. Eventually, however, through her growing friendship with Chan and Hunt, she comes to reorient and reanchor her life: from seeking an ultimate freedom she turns to seeking a place within a supportive family and community. It is neither an easy nor a quick reorientation, but her growing love for Hunt—and his reciprocal feelings—prod her toward seeing the emptiness and selfishness underlying a radical freedom that leaves her unconnected to others. "Other people," she had said at one point before her change of heart, "they complicate everything, but if you can cut loose from even the last one you can start over. One part dies and the larger part comes to life" (HW 188). Later, now moving toward a commitment with Hunt, she sees that he is right when he says that to live alone is less liberating than lonely, that being alone leads to stasis and a hardening of self, that personal growth comes through interactions with and commitments to others. Although Nancy resists this knowledge at first—she would much rather believe in the Western legend of bountiful freedom and endless possibility—she knows instinctively the wisdom of Hunt's words. When she first sees the Grand Canyon, she jerks back speechless, realizing that the gaping emptiness of the abyss mirrors the abyss to which she is headed in trying to empty herself of her past and of other people.

Like Judge Jolley, who returns home to face a criminal indictment, Nancy in the end returns home to deal with the situation she left behind. But she is not returning to step again into her old roles as librarian and family martyr but rather to organize her affairs so she can leave again, this time by her own choice. Her second journey west will not be a reckless bolt for freedom but a deliberate decision to be a part of family and community, to settle down with Hunt.

Nancy's renewal and regeneration, it turns out, thus come less in her showdown with Dwight than in her showdown with Hunt. Although the duel with Dwight in the Grand Canyon is no doubt significant in her development, what carries her finally forward to wholeness is her decision not merely to walk away, not merely to forget, not merely to keep on heading west and leaving everything she has done behind her. Unlike the men in *Deliverance*, who bury their experiences — and their victims — and walk away from any responsibility for what they have done, Nancy confronts the significance of her acts, even returning to Dwight's family to discover more about him and to let his family that know that he is dead. Such actions are part of her renewal and growth, as manifested in conscience and in responsibility both to herself and to others.

At the end of *Heading West*, Nancy pushes aside a set of alabaster monkeys on the family mantelpiece — the three monkeys who can neither see, speak, nor hear evil — in order to see in the mirror "the last monkey — herself — who could do evil and know it" (HW 368). Nancy's vacation from conscience and responsibility is over. She's ready to embrace her individual and community identities; her joining up with Hunt suggests a happy merging of these identities and a balancing of her desires to nest and to fly. Their pending marriage will in all likelihood mirror the balance and happiness of Chan and Richard's. "The marriage was happy," the narrator relates. "They balanced each other's extremes: Chan, who could read courage and honor into the reflexes of every dog; against Richard, who saw beyond every human action the power of surviving instincts and animal hungers. Without her he would have grown cold and melancholy; she, in another setting, might have been all gush and baby talk. Between them some vaporous Golden Mean shimmered in the domestic air" (HW 182–83). The golden dream of heading west has become in the end the golden mean of marriage, a balancing of love, commitment, and freedom. Or more simply, the best of the West and the best of the South.

In Betts's second novel about heading west, *The Sharp Teeth of*

Love (1997), two characters, Luna and Paul, also move toward achieving a similar domestic balance of freedom and commitment. But before they do, they have much to experience and learn. Luna is going west with her fiancé, Steven, who has taken a job in California; but on the drive out, she runs away from him, having come to see the destructiveness of the relationship, how much Steven has been feeding off and on her. Like Nancy in *Heading West*, when Luna bolts, she is seeking to free herself from people and obligations. She has spent most of her life trying to please others, particularly her father and Steven, and she relishes being alone, "cut loose from people, obligations."[3] Paul Cowan, on the other hand, has come west after a spiritual crisis; he hopes to discover himself and his faith in the visionary world of California. Yet he is terribly disappointed, finding California spiritually empty; religion there, he says, is less rigorous faith than comforting mood, "profess[ing] at most two Commandments plus maybe eight Suggestions" (STL 258). Adding to his isolation and alienation, an accident has left him almost completely deaf.

Looming over Luna's and Paul's quests are several terrifying situations that cast dark shadows on their efforts. Shadowing Paul's search for a religious grounding and community is the shoot-out at Waco, Texas, between federal agents and David Koresh and his followers. Koresh's messianic cult points to the destructive extreme that lonely, alienated individuals can reach in their search for meaning and purpose. Shadowing Luna's quest for independence are two ominous occurrences: the cannibalism that occurred at Donner Pass during the winter of 1846–47, and the sexual abuse of the young boy, Sam, whom Luna befriends while camping. Luna finds herself driven to understand the events that transpired during the Donner expedition, particularly the choice made by Tamsen Donner to stay behind and take care of her dying husband, who apparently had no chance of survival — a choice that led to her own death. Tamsen's choice not to save herself, together with her later cannibalization, points to the extreme to which relationships can go when one member sacrifices everything for the other. Similarly the fate of Sam, a boy abducted to become a child prostitute, points to the extreme result of radical freedom — a Darwinistic world in which everyone is fending for himself and herself, the strongest surviving and oppressing the weaker.

Through their combined efforts to save Sam and their growing love for each other, Luna and Paul both come to realize the destructive lengths to which their flights could possibly take them. They come to see that beneath the myth of the legendary cowboy West — of living free and easy, in terms of both individual and spiritual freedom — lies a brutal "dog-eat-dog terrain where the Brass Rule — *Do or be done to* — prevailed" (STL 115). At the novel's end, Luna, Paul, and Sam are heading *eastward* to start a new life together, joined together in a happy combination of love, commitment, and self-preservation, a balance similar to the one forged by Nancy and Hunt in Betts's *Heading West*. While there is still talk of eating flesh and religious faith, it is in terms not of cannibalization and cults but of the Eucharist and marriage. They are headed to Paul's home in Wisconsin, in the Midwest — a place suggesting the balance between the East and the West, the balance between conflicting pulls of commitment and freedom that Paul and Luna together have now reconciled.

Betts is not alone in pushing toward a golden mean founded in marriage and relationships that balances the westering impulse toward flight and individual freedom with the impulse to settle down and root oneself in place. Indeed, a number of male writers follow her lead, focusing on characters (usually male) who face situations and conflicts similar to those of Betts's protagonists. Given the mythic models available to men—particularly those celebrating the frontiersman and the rugged individualist—the desire to live in motion appears stronger in much of these male writers' works, and thus the tension between moving on and nesting is especially great, one that at times takes Herculean efforts to resolve.

Nowhere is this tension more evident than in Chris Offutt's *The Same River Twice* (1993), a memoir of his days of wandering and eventual settling down as husband and father. Told in chapters that alternate between Offutt's youthful life on the road and his later settling down, the memoir is given a helix structure that embodies the two pulls within Offutt's life, which are brought into healthy balance only near the close of the text. The chapters dealing with his flight portray Offutt's desire to live unencumbered and uncommitted, without ties to others or to the past; as he characterizes himself, he "was a perpetual new face," hitchhiking from one place to another without direction or purpose, living by "random patterns of oblique and gleeful entropy."[4] Whenever his life begins in any way to get complicated, it is time to pick up and leave "like Daniel Boone for elbow room" (SRT 44).

Offutt's mention of Boone points to his close identification with the early pioneer and his wandering life. Himself born and raised in the Daniel Boone National Forest in the Appalachian Mountains of Kentucky, Offutt repeatedly invokes Boone to justify his wanderlust. When he bolts from Minneapolis, knowing fully well that staying would mean the risk of being tied down in marriage, Offutt says he departs because "the ghost of Daniel whispered that I should leave" (53). Reenacting the legend of Boone, of picking up stakes when people get too close—for Offutt, it is when people get too close emotionally—is the only structure underpinning Offutt's life, itself less a structure than a resistance to structure.

The other pioneer figure haunting Offutt's youth is Christopher Columbus, another hero of westward movement—and a destroyer of tradition and community, the type of explorer Allen Tate complains of in "The Mediterranean." As he does with Boone, Offutt invokes Columbus to justify his own wanderings and, specifically, his leaving home. Offutt configures himself as a modern-day Columbus driven to discover new worlds, pushing from the known to the unknown, living by adventure rather than safety and security. Comparing himself to his brother Dane, a mathematician whose "life moved along an advanced formula of direct lines, bracketed exponents, congruent functions, and the ultimate goal of symmetry," Offutt declares: "Dane could prove the world was round without ever leaving his room. I needed wind, a flagship, and open water" (SRT 121). Even a brief, and reluctant, return home for Dane's wedding makes Offutt feel constricted: "after Columbus's third trip across the sea, he was brought home in manacles and chains. I knew how he felt" (122). He also suggests he knows how Columbus felt in the presence of the king. Contrasting himself with his father, whom he sees during this visit home, Offutt says that "he was Ferdinand ruling Portugal, and he could keep it. I had the New World" (123).

Eventually, however, Offutt begins to weary of his wandering and to see the emptiness of what he now understands as his directionless— and far from heroic—life. Helping him reach this understanding is his realization that the West, rather than being a place of rebirth and transfiguration, is merely one more stop along the way. "The legendary West, with its vast and empty spaces," Offutt writes, "had boiled down to just that—vast and empty, filled with people trying desperately to plug the gap with labor" (SRT 71). He comes to see that the motto by which he has lived, "Always Forward," has not been carrying him forward at all; he sees that he has always been running *from* rather than *toward* something and that after years of travel he has gone nowhere. Rather than as an explorer with purpose and direction, he now sees himself as an exile, adrift and purposeless. He is not, finally, as he had once thought, Columbus discovering a new world but "Columbus lost in the fog" (120).

Offutt comes out of his fog when he heads to Boston to reconnect with an old friend, the first time during all his years of journeying that he has ever returned to any place. His coming back to Boston signals the end of his exile and the beginning of his life within the human community. Not long afterward, he meets Rita, and his open-road roaming comes to an end in marriage and fatherhood. He is no longer Boone the trail breaker but Boone the family man, the frontiersman who repeatedly took to the woods but always doubled back home to his family. This motion out and back—rather than the motion continuously out—now becomes Offutt's model for living: from his home, the center point of his life, he takes solitary walks out into the woods, not to flee responsibilities and commitments but to prepare himself better for accepting and following through on the demands of family life. Not only does he collect his thoughts and energies on his walks, but he discovers in the woods models for his new life. On a walk at the spring equinox, for example, Offutt sees in the woods "the beginning of life and crop, of nesting birds and mating animals" (SRT 188). Once a space of isolation and reckless freedom, the wilderness now is for Offutt a place of procreation and community, a model not of wandering but of settling in.

At the end of *The Same River Twice*, with his son in his arms, Offutt walks in the woods and observes that "the river flows beside us and touching it means touching the sea" (SRT 188). Once believing he always needed to be on open water, always on a voyage out, Offutt now understands he can be can have that freedom anywhere, even at home. He knows that he now carries *within* him the wildness of river and sea, a knowledge underscored by the title of Richard Hugo's poem that Offutt quotes as his memoir's epigraph—"The Towns We Know and Leave Behind, the Rivers We Carry with Us."

The charged tension between family responsibility and individual freedom also shapes Offutt's novel, *The Good Brother* (1997). Here a young Kentuckian, Virgil Caudill, is pressured by his family and community to avenge the killing of his brother, an act that would ironically doom Virgil to exile from the very community that demands action. Virgil does eventually murder his brother's killer, Rodale, thus becoming in the community's eyes "the good brother"; he then takes flight west, ending up deep in the Montana woods. Here Virgil dreams of putting the past entirely and safely behind him, hoping to live free and unencumbered, a new man in a new world. But as so many other characters in Southern fiction discover, fleeing the burdens of history and responsibility does not mean freeing oneself of them. Indeed, Virgil's flight westward reveals to him not only the impossibility and irresponsibility of cutting oneself off from family and community but also the terrifying extremes to which the dream of freedom can take one.

Virgil's efforts at remaking himself in Montana primarily involve making sure he is wearing the right disguise. He assumes the new name Joe Tiller, wears the proper clothes, drives the right kind of car, walks with the correct swagger. But while Virgil can successfully persuade others that he is a man of the West—that is, a rugged individualist with no ties to anyone other than himself—he soon realizes he cannot fool himself. His identity is too grounded in Kentucky, in place, for him to be at home in Montana. A profound dissatisfaction almost immediately cuts deep into Virgil's elation at his escape and move west. Right after his forthright declaration of his new Montanan identity, "My name is Joe Tiller and this is where I live," he more soberly admits his radical displacement, declaring to himself that "this was not his world."[5] Later he echoes this observation with the admission that "this land's not mine. It's great to look at, but it's not part of me" (GB 302).

It is no doubt in large part Virgil's failure to put behind him his life in Kentucky — and all that this life represents in terms of placement within a family and community — that gives him a perspective for understanding the limitations and dangers of Western individualism. Indeed, it does not take long before Virgil sees that despite its celebrating individual rights and autonomy, the backwoods Montana culture where he lives is in many ways as rigidly exclusionary and hierarchical as the most closed Southern society. Race and pedigree — in terms both of class and of time in residence — determine one's rank in Montana society, as the narrator reports Virgil (now calling himself Joe) thinking: "Everyone tried to compete for a Montana degree. It began with old families and worked its way down to the recent arrivals. The longer you'd been in the state, the more deserving you were of living there. Each group of newcomers resented the next and everyone conveniently left the Indians out of the equation. It seemed to Joe that people forgot Americans were allowed to live anywhere in the country, including Montana" (GB 156). Such are the rigid markers structuring the cult(ure) of Western individualism.

The dangers of radical individualism are most visible in the paramilitary survivalists, the Bills, who reject all government authority and form a secret society closed to all who do not look, act, and think as they do.[6] While espousing individual freedom, the Bills ironically demand that members completely subsume their identities into the group. From an ideology based on liberty, the Bills establish a social structure that mirrors their own worst nightmare: a totalitarian organization headed by an iron-fisted dictator. And just as ironically, the Bills draw their numbers from the victims of a fragmented Western culture that downplays the community for the individual; isolated and alienated people, individuals adrift, look to the Bills for a family and community they cannot find elsewhere in the West.

It is precisely the possibility of regrounding himself within family and community that initially draws Virgil to the Bills, despite his recoiling from their extremist views. He wants what living alone in the woods does not offer — sharing comfort in relationships and community. How much Virgil misses such grounding becomes explosively clear when he confronts Orben, the man on a mission to avenge Virgil's murder of Rodale. Frank feels an instant connection with his fellow Kentuckian, despite the fact that Orben is there to kill him. After catching up on news from the home place, Virgil talks about the futility and purposelessness of his displaced life, admitting about the shooting that "not a day goes by that I don't wish I never done it" (GB 301). He goes on to describe all that he misses — his family, his friends, the land, the talk — less to save himself than to save Orben from the life of a fugitive. Through their conversation, Virgil eventually guides Orben away from his mission of vengeance.

By the end of the novel, Virgil the good brother has become Virgil the lost brother. As federal agents close in, Virgil dreams of taking flight to Alaska, despite knowing how little that dream has to offer. Heading west, he knows now, offers not new beginnings but merely fanciful illusions; the possibility of further flight west is merely a "last resort, like poison that a terminal patient keeps handy" (GB 262). Virgil knows that cutting oneself off from one's community carries a psychological burden much more destructive and confining than whatever demands a community makes for conformity. As Offutt himself learned in his own travels west, the legendary West is indeed legendary — a world of fanciful dreams masking the vast emptiness of the landscape and the broken lives of individuals who have escaped there vainly looking for better things.

Besides dreaming of lighting out to Alaska, Virgil imagines of what would have happened had he stayed in Kentucky and not killed Rodale. Of course, Virgil's musings are as fanciful as the dream of Western freedom, but that dream of making do within a community haunts *The Good Brother,* and certainly it is clear that creating space *within* family and community is more rewarding than seeking space outside them. It is too late for Virgil to swing home and find his place; he lost that chance in his act of violence. But the promise of settling in, rather than taking flight, is finally what *The Good Brother* affirms. Even if it is only in Virgil's dreams, the line heading westward becomes in the end the circle that heads back home, just as it does in Betts's fiction.

Rick Bass, the contemporary Southern writer who has most enthusiastically embraced the wilderness as a guiding force in life and art, is much more positive than Betts and Offutt about the value of individual freedom. In the end, though, he too embraces a circling back, a balance between home and solitude, responsibility and freedom. For Bass, moving west is a stepping free in every sense of the word, a move toward independence and a commitment to live by the elemental wildness embedded within us all. As suggested by the title of his collection of autobiographical essays, *Wild to the Heart* (1987), Bass believes that all people carry within them a fundamental wildness — a spirit of joy, wonder, and hope that mirrors the rhythms of the natural world and that is being crushed by the demands and routines of everyday contemporary life. *Wild to the Heart* chronicles Bass's efforts to keep that wildness vital. Although he feels most alive when he is camping in the Utah mountains, Bass eventually comes to see that wildness and freedom depend more on vision than on location. "If you focus on the right things, and ignore the others," Bass writes, "you can find wildness and freedom anywhere."[7] Armed with this Weltyesque knowledge of sight and insight, Bass makes a stirring call for others to embrace and nurture the wilderness of their interior lives: "If it's wild to your own heart, protect it. Preserve it. Love it. And fight for it, and dedicate yourself to it, whether it's a mountain range, your wife, your husband, or even (heaven forbid) your job. It doesn't matter if it's wild to anyone else: if it's what makes your heart sing, if it's what makes your days soar like a hawk in the summertime, then focus on it. Because for sure, it's wild, and if it's wild, it'll mean you're still free. No matter where you are" (WH 158).

Although here downplaying place in his celebration of vision, Bass in his later works celebrates a particular place — the wilderness West — as imperative for him to maintain his joy and freedom. Vision and focus are of course still important, but the West, specifically Montana's Yaak Valley, nourishes and grounds the wholeness and insight Bass seeks. In *Winter: Notes from Montana* (1991), Bass describes himself and his wife, Elizabeth, as modern-day pioneers, made world-weary by the routines of modern life, gripped by the dream of renewing themselves in the West. Merely getting in the car to drive west makes Bass feel "freer and fresher and more daring, more hopeful than I can ever remember feeling."[8]

Later, when Elizabeth arrives, Bass declares the break with the past complete. "All the rest of our old life fell away into the past," he writes, adding that "it was intoxicating to have nothing behind us anymore, and to have everything ahead of us" (W 15). In a hopeful and unironic dismissal of the past, rare in Southern writing, Bass here wholeheartedly embraces the American dream of leaving history behind, of fleeing west into a new world of possibility and potentiality.

It is the dream that, as Bass notes in *The Book of Yaak* (1996), "seems to be the genetic predisposition in our country's blood—the handwriting of it telling us to move across the country from right to left, always farther from some echo of England, perhaps, or farther from everything."[9]

When Bass first drives into Montana's Purcell Mountains, he says that it was like "wading into cold water on a fall day" (w 7). Here and elsewhere, Bass characterizes moving to the West as a bracing immersion in a frigid lake or stream, a shocking bodily awakening from the enervating life left behind in modern society. Bass typically depicts modern urban life in terms of incarceration, people locked away in "high-rise jails" and ensnared in smothering routines.[10] "Sometimes I feel," the narrator of Bass's story "Swamp Boy" says, "as if I've become so entombed that I have *become* the giant building in which I work—that it is my shell, my exoskeleton, like the seashell in which a fiddler crab lives, hauling the stiff burden of it around for the rest of his days" (ILM 27–28). While Bass has little good to say about modern life in any region, he finds that life in the South is particularly grim, since not only has the region embraced New South corporatism and boosterism but it also has remained shackled by an overwhelming sense of history. "Nothing is forgotten," the narrator of Bass's short story "Mississippi" comments, characterizing Southern history's stranglehold upon the region.[11]

So strong is history's grip that Bass suggests that history even permeates the South's natural world. The narrator of "Government Bears" notes the lingering presence of the Civil War in Southern woods:

I don't care if it was a hundred and twenty years ago, these things still last and that is really no time at all, not for a real war like that one, with screaming and pain. The trees absorb the echoes of the screams and cries and humiliations. Their bark is only an inch thick between the time then and now: the distance between your thumb and forefinger. The sun beating down on us now saw the flames and troops' campfires then, and in fact the warmth from those flames is still not entirely through traveling to the sun. The fear of the women: you can still feel it, in places where it was strong. (TW 172–73)

In contrast to the Southern woods, Bass conceives the Western wilderness as being free from history, a point underscored in his conceptualization of his move to Montana as a crossing from the historical (modernity and linear time) into the natural (nature and lunar cycles). In this regard, Bass's image of plunging into frigid water implies not only the cleansing that comes in moving West—to enter the wilderness is to wash off the grime of civilization, bodily as well as spiritually—but also the invigoration of being freed from the burden of history.

Immersion also suggests, even more significantly, regeneration. For Bass, moving to the West involves the shedding of the burdensome and confining shell of modern identity. As he puts it in *Winter*: "I felt like I'd wanted my entire life to peel off my city ways, city life, and get into the woods—molting, like an insect or a snake (160). To live in the Western wilderness is to embrace humanity's "natural" state of being; it is to reorient one's life according to the cycles of the natural world, what Bass calls "the blood-rhythms of wilderness" (BY 13). Masked and repressed by modern culture, these rhythms live deep within the hearts of humanity, ready to be drawn out and nurtured. Early in *The Book of Yaak*, Bass asks "is it too much to imagine that the pulsings of our blood, and our emotions, follow the rough profile of the days of light in this valley?" (3). He goes on to describe how his body has been slowing adapting to the wilderness patterns: "My blood began to learn new rhythms. My body became increasingly fluent in the language of cycles. . . . Small cycles radiated into larger ones. I kept following them — noticing different ones each day — and continue to." Bass comes to realize these reorientations are fitting him to the wilderness, giving him his place. He is, he notes, "being reshaped and refashioned, to better fit it in spirit and desire" (BY 5–6).

Bass elsewhere depicts these transformations in terms of a positively configured devolution, a descent that by his yardstick is actually an ascent — a far cry from the bestiality into which characters in Cormac McCarthy's work frequently devolve — toward the primal state of the animal. "I'm falling away from the human race," Bass writes in *Winter*. "I don't mean to sound churlish — but I'm liking it. It frightens me a little to recognize how much I like it. It's as if you'd looked down at your hand and seen the beginnings of fur. It's not as bad as you might think" (W 73). In *The Book of Yaak* he experiences an initial uneasiness about his growing adaptation to the wilderness, feeling himself "a misanthrope, turning back and away from the human race." "I was more ape than man," he writes. "I had shaken off old human loyalties." After a time, however, the uneasiness gives way to joyful acceptance, since "the truth is the truth, and after a while it didn't matter" (BY 21). At the end of *Winter* Bass is at his most definitive regarding his transformations: "I admire the weasels, the rabbits, and the other wild creatures that can change with the seasons, that can change almost overnight. It's taken me a long time to change completely — thirty years — but now I've changed. I don't have any interest in turning back. I won't be leaving this valley" (W 162)

Bass's falling away from the human, of course, does not carry him entirely into the animal realm — animals do not embark on quests to understand themselves, nor do they write books. Moreover, in the Montana woods Bass does not live alone, without human connection; he is there with Elizabeth and their two sons — and his home is clearly his gravitational center. Less the misanthrope than the family man, Bass in his efforts at psychological wholeness resembles Chris Offutt in *The Same River Twice:* both seek to balance the urge toward wilderness freedom with the pull toward home. Like Offutt's, Bass's solitary walks into the woods are not flights from but lessons in community. Bass sees modern life as a "lost-gyroscopic tumble" (BY xv) of greed and rapacity, with the wilderness as a counterforce of stability, a place of "unrelenting order and complexity, unrelenting grace" (BY 181). Rather than seeing the natural world as a bloody Darwinian battlefield, which is what modern corporate society has become, Bass sees it as the model of the self-supporting community by which he structures his own life. A triple-trunked larch tree, standing only with the help of its neighbors, becomes for Bass the image of nature's community: "Trees of different species formed a circle around it — fir, aspen, lodgepole, even cedar. Their branches, as it was growing, must have helped to shelter and stabilize it, hold it up, as though they were friends, or at the very least — and in the sense of the word that I think we must turn to the woods to relearn — like community" (BY 181).

The issues that Bass foregrounds in his nonfiction about living in the West — particularly matters involving self-renewal and regeneration — profoundly shape his fiction. Bass's stories characteristically explore the conflicting urges toward settling down in a community and lighting out into a space of individual freedom. Although Bass typically valorizes the compulsion to break through the nets of conformity and standardization, to move psychologically if not literally to the West, he makes it clear that both compulsions at their extremes push one toward self-destruction: living within a community, one can become rigid and repressed; living with complete individual freedom, one can become isolated and misanthropic.

Those characters in Bass's fiction who take flight from confinement — usually manifested in a smothering marriage or relationship — typically enjoy a life of unfettered freedom for only so long. After being alone for a while, they usually find themselves drawn back toward others, sometimes into new relationships, sometimes to the very situation from which they bolted. In "The Myth of Bears," for instance, Judith flees into the wilderness to escape her husband, Trapper, only to realize her need to feel connected to Trapper even as she flees him. As much as she likes to be on the run, she realizes that she enjoys her freedom only when she knows that Trapper is pursuing her. "It's terrible without the thought of him out there chasing her, hunting her," the narrator reports her thinking. "It's horrible. There's too much space."[12] After Trapper eventually catches up with Judith, they return to home together, quickly settling into their old routines. At the end, Judith remains caught between her conflicting pulls of settling in and escaping, though at least for now the tension is no longer so wrenching as to be destructive. "She feels cut in half," the narrator observes, "but strangely, there is no pain" (ssw 45). The challenge facing characters such as Judith is to find a way to live independently — to feel free — while at the same time being involved with another person and/or other people. Negotiating this space between freedom and confinement — this psychological frontier — is the task with which most of Bass's characters struggle.

Truly lost are those characters in Bass's fiction who do not respond to the challenge to integrate freedom within community. They remain paralyzed, frozen in place by the security and comfort of inertia. Not only destructive to themselves, they frequently seek to hold back others, psychologically, if not literally, in their little worlds. Hollingsworth, for instance, in "The Watch" ends up chaining his father to the porch of their home to keep the old man from taking off to live in a community of runaways deep in the swamp. Some characters, like Hollingsworth, never come to understand the destruction they inflict as they strive to keep things fixed and unchanging. Others come to see their failings, like Harley in "Platte River," who in the end understands that he has always been constrained by the past, that he has never been able to let anything go or to live without restraint. Living as he has, he sees, has turned him "into a fucking *crustacean*," burdened and burdensome.[13] At the story's end, he stands at the Pacific coast and feels for the first time the urge to take flight, imagining the joyous possibilities of hopping aboard an outbound ship and riding it to wherever it is going. It is just such a freedom that Bass everywhere celebrates; it is the joyful wildness buried deep within humanity, the wildness that is nowhere more outwardly manifested than in Bass's beloved Montana wilderness, the wilderness that he, in his role as environmental activist, is working tirelessly to save.

Richard Ford's Montana has little of the joy that Rick Bass's does. Although sharing with Bass a poignant awareness of the need for human connection, Ford depicts a West that is the inverse of Bass's, a negative of his photograph. For the most part Ford's West is cheerless and enervating, less a place of new beginnings and rebirth than of boredom and gloom. Most of his stories take place either in late fall, with winter looming, or in the dead of winter; there is a sense of winding down toward death or, even more depressingly, of living a death-in-life. Ford's West might be encapsulated in the opening of his short story "Great Falls": "This is not a happy story. I warn you."[14]

The people who inhabit Ford's West are unhappy in part because of the emptiness of their lives, an emptiness that is mirrored in the landscape itself. Life in this barren region stands in sharp contrast to that in the suburban East. As we see in *The Sportswriter* and *Independence Day*, suburban life prompts people to appreciate the everyday and the familiar. Frank Bascombe finds the daily routines of the suburbs comforting and nurturing, and so he judges the attractiveness of a place by its ordinariness. Perhaps most significantly for Frank, the suburbs do not prompt false illusions about the grandeur of life:

> Better to come to earth in New Jersey than not to come at all. Or worse, to come to your senses in some spectral place like Colorado or California, or to remain up in the dubious airs searching for some right place that never existed and never will. Stop searching. Face the earth where you can. Literally speaking, it's all you have to go on. Indeed, in its homeliest precincts and turn-outs, the state feels as unpretentious as Cape Cod once might've, and its bustling suburban-with-good-neighbor-industry mix of life makes it the quintessence of the town-and-country spirit. Illusion will never be your adversary here.[15]

The ordinary life of the suburbs, what Frank characterizes as "a pleasant, easy existence," is one that "stanched almost any kind of unhappiness" (SW 225).

All this security in the ordinary contrasts sharply with what Frank sees as the lure of the "spectral" West, the American dream, as manifested in the wide-open West, which fosters wild-eyed illusions of grandeur and fulfillment. In this hopeful—and finally woeful—dream, happiness lies always somewhere just down the road. "Americans always feel like the real life is somewhere else," Frank says (SW 158), and so they miss the value of the world that is around them. For Frank, the capacity for stability and happiness lies in the ability to see the wonder in the familiar and ordinary, and so one of his favorite pastimes is going to a suburban train station to witness the trains and the commuters on their way. "There is mystery everywhere, even in a vulgar, urine-scented, suburban depot such as this," declares Frank. "You have only to let yourself in for it. You can never know what's coming next. Always there is the chance it will be — miraculous to say — something you want" (sw 342).

For this reason Frank would rather look at merchandise catalogs than, say, a book of Ansel Adams photographs, since the catalogs ground him in the everyday, fostering "an odd assurance that some things outside my life were okay still; that the same men and women standing by the familiar brick fireplaces, or by the same comfortable canopy beds, holding these same shotguns or blow poles or boot warmers or boxes of kindling sticks could see a good day before their eyes right into perpetuity. Things were knowable, safe-and-sound. Everybody with exactly what they need or could get. A perfect illustration of how the literal can become the mildly mysterious" (sw 196). As Frank observes, it is better to locate one's life in the small and the everyday and to find comfort there than to pursue grand illusions. "Whose life ever has permanent mystery built into it anyway?" he asks. "An astronaut? The heavyweight champ? A Ubangi tribesman?" (350).

Although Bascombe realizes the impossibility of a life of permanent wonder, he is certainly open to moments of wonder and to the *possibility* of wondrous change. Frank categorizes people into two groups according to their approaches to life. Literalists are those who enjoy the world in which they find themselves, content with what is literally there; a literalist, for example, would "enjoy watching people while stranded in an airport" (sw 133). Factualists, on the other hand, care less about the literal than they do about understanding why the literal is as it is and what it all means. The factualist stranded in an airport, Frank notes, "can't stop wondering why his plane was late out of Salt Lake, and gauging whether they'll serve dinner or just a snack" (133). A healthy life somehow brings literalism and factualism into balance, so that a person not only remains grounded in the literal but also seeks larger understanding of his or her life. To be completely literal is to be mired in details that do not connect, to live entirely in the present, the world governed by chance and accident. To be entirely factual is to lose grounding in the real, to search endlessly for explanations and answers, the presence of the immediate world slipping away.

For the most part, life in Ford's Montana seems gripped by a destructive literalism. In *Rock Springs, Wildlife,* and the novella "Jealous" from *Women with Men,* characters suffer from the sense that nothing much matters, that one experience is merely one more experience in a patternless run of experiences. There is a dreary flatness of feeling, even in situations such as youthful sex and the breakup of families in which one would expect emotional responses spiking off the chart. In "Children," after his friend has had sex with a girl with whom they've been cruising, the narrator comments that "what we did . . . didn't matter so much. Not to us, or to anyone. She might've have been with me instead of Claude, or with Claude's father, or another man none of us knew" (RS 95). In "Empire," after sleeping with a neighbor while his wife lies desperately ill in the hospital, Sims dismisses his adultery by saying that "there was no use letting anything bother him. This was not his life and wouldn't ever be. None of it made any sense, but it didn't make any difference, either. Months from then, if Marge lived, he'd tell her about it and they'd have a big laugh together" (RS 131). Here is the primary danger of extreme literalism: people close down their lives, abandoning goals and purpose, living only for the moment and often being bored even with that.

At its extreme, literalism represents the dark underside of American individualism and the Western legend of possibility and opportunity. Since nothing much matters in a world of random occurrences, the literalist tends to walk away from anything bothersome, not burdened by any responsibility for whatever has happened. People in Ford's West frequently do just that, leaving unhappy homes to look for new lives in what they envision as a world of uncharted freedom. Those fleeing, however, usually find little in their journeys other than deep-seated regret and loneliness, manifested in strings of unsatisfying relationships and restless waywardness. Moreover, their flights for freedom usually bring terrible suffering to those left behind. Ford's West is littered with the debris of broken families.

Eventually most of Ford's Western literalists abandon their literalism in seeking to understand their lives, but this turnaround usually comes long after the events that have crucially shaped their lives. Most of Ford's Western fiction is told retrospectively, with narrators, once literalists who rarely looked beyond the immediate, now factualists struggling to make sense of their complicated lives. They have swung from one extreme to the other, embodying now as storytellers what Ford elsewhere calls "idiotic factualism or the indignity of endless explanation" (SW 206). They are now entirely ensnared by their pasts, so fixated by previous events that their present lives have all but ground to a halt — except for their musings on the past. "Explaining is where we all get into trouble," says Frank Bascombe (SW 223), and this is the trouble plaguing most of the narrators of Ford's Western fiction.

The way out of this ensnarement is easy to articulate but hard to put into practice: let go of the past, particularly the painful and discouraging times. That is exactly what Ford's narrators cannot do, even when they want to, and their failure represents another of Ford's swipes at the illusory nature of the American dream, the dream of being unburdened by the past. The narrator of "Rock Springs," a very unsuccessful man, rightly conjectures that successful people are successful in part because they can easily forget troublesome times, moving on with their lives instead of endlessly analyzing them. Frank Bascombe, back in New Jersey, also knows the value of forgetting. He knows that wallowing in the past fosters regretful self-absorption and, even worse, cynicism. As Frank observes, "there is no cynicism like lifelong self-love and the tunnel vision in which you yourself are all that's visible at the tunnel's end" (sw 172). The routine of sportswriting — of getting new assignments, of starting each interview and article fresh — becomes Frank's model for a happy life. As he notes contentedly about his career and life, "I have a clean slate almost every day of my life, a chance not to be negative, to give someone unknown a pat on the back, to recognize courage and improvement, to take the battle with cynicism head-on and win" (sw 152).

Forgetting for Ford does not mean wiping the slate completely clean; to forget everything would plunge a person into extreme literalism, the world back to appearing endlessly new, endlessly random. Forgetting for Ford means breaking the past's stranglehold upon the consciousness so that one is not forever tied to what has gone before; it is the first step in striking the balance between literalism and factualism that allows a person to move forward in life but with discretion, judgment, and responsibility. Striking such a balance is immensely difficult, even for a tremendously self-aware man like Frank, who by and large knows what he wants from life and how to get it. One notes, for instance, that despite all his commentary on the value of forgetting, Frank narrates in *The Sportswriter* and *Independence Day* about nine hundred pages of densely packed prose about himself. Very, very little has been forgotten, and there is a tremendous amount of self-analysis.

That Frank remembers so much yet remains so vitally alive suggests that he is moving toward, and perhaps even achieving, the type of balance in his life that people in Ford's West find so elusive. Crucial to forging this balance is accepting one's past without letting it solidify into a rock-hard monolith that cannot be revised, altered, or, if need be, forgotten. For Frank, nothing is permanent, not even the past, which lives in memories that must continually be rethought and reevaluated if one is to achieve a rich and fulfilling life. Remembering involves critical thinking and choice, including the choice of forgetting. "Some things can't be explained," Frank says. "They just are. And after a while they disappear, usually forever, or become interesting in another way. . . . It is better not even to look so hard, to leave off explaining. Nothing makes me more queasy than to spend time with people who don't know that and who can't forget, and for whom such knowledge isn't a cornerstone of life" (sw 223–24).

The narrators in Ford's West rarely reach such a balanced understanding of themselves, instead swinging wildly between a hard-core literalism and a hard-core factualism, both of which embody an ungenerous, if not mean-spirited, selfishness. This overwhelming focus on self represents the souring of the American dream of individualism and independence; in Ford's West that dream has degenerated, as the narrator of "Great Falls" puts it, into "just low-life, some coldness in us all, some helplessness that causes us to misunderstand life when it is pure and plain, makes our existence seem like a border between two nothings, and makes us no more or less than animals who meet on the road — watchful, unforgiving, without patience or desire" (rs 49). The narrator's comment in "Children" that his endless thinking only of himself has made him "bitter and lonesome and useless" (RS 96) speaks for the predicament of most of the characters in Ford's West, almost all of whom never get beyond their selfishness, if they ever even acknowledge it.

One exception occurs at the end of *Wildlife*, when Joe's mother, who has had an affair and left her family, returns home to mend things and start over. It is one of the few times in Ford's Western fiction that characters attempt to reconstruct shattered lives and families, and the passage is worth quoting:

> And then at the end of March, in 1961, just as it was beginning to be spring, my mother came back from wherever she had been. In a while she and my father found a way to settle the difficulties that had been between them. And though they may both have felt that something had died between them, something they may not even have been aware of until it was gone and disappeared from their lives forever, they must've felt — both of them — that there was something of themselves, something important, that could not live at all in any other way but by their being together, much as they had been before. I do not know exactly what that something was.[16]

If not marital bliss, there are understanding and sharing here, a coming together that is indeed "something important," a rebonding and rebuilding.

Ford certainly does not celebrate family and community as wholeheartedly as Betts, Offutt, and Bass, but the ideal of family and community nonetheless looms large in Ford's work, even in its absence. This absence defines much of the sadness of his fiction: knowing fully well the value of family and commitment, people in Ford's West cannot find it in their own lives, or are not willing to work for it, or deliberately destroy it, or yearn for a time when their lives had it, or bitterly remember when their lives came undone in an act of betrayal. Happiness does not come easily in this bleak world, but one thing does seem clear: it is best to stay put and work to make things better rather than moving on when things go bad. That is what the narrator of "Great Falls" finally comes to know: "Things can be fixed by staying; but to go out into the night and not come back hazards life, and everything can get out of hand" (RS 48).

Things certainly get out of hand, at least for a while, in Frederick Barthelme's *Painted Desert* (1995), a novel about two modern-day vigilantes-to-be heading west—and a novel, I need to add, that differs dramatically from Barthelme's other work. Barthelme characteristically writes about the glitzy and kitschy suburbs of the Mississippi Gulf Coast, where everyday suburban people struggle with everyday suburban problems. Characters rarely feel the urge to pick up and head west—except metaphorically, that is—in the urge to start over in a new life. Cutting loose usually means moving across town, not driving into the sunset down I-10. In Barthelme's postmodern suburbs, place has very little significance, with one place resembling every other place and with the web of media and telecommunications, upon which everyone thrives, stretching everywhere. What difference, finally, does it make where a person lives in Barthelme's postmodern suburbia? Not much, particularly since most of his characters live almost entirely by their workday routines and the TV schedule. When they feel the urge to search for the wondrous, they resemble the questers in Madison Smartt Bell, looking for it in the smallest details of the world about them—for instance, in glistening asphalt or in pork chops sizzling on the grill, details that can be found anywhere.

In *Painted Desert*, however, two characters, Del and Jen, decide to leave the Gulf Coast behind and to strike out for the West. Enraged by scenes they have seen on TV depicting the riots after the trial of the assailants of Rodney King, they vow to clean up the streets of Los Angeles, using violence if necessary, or so they say (they never get close to any weapons). "It's important for us to take a stand," Jen says. "We need to demonstrate that certain behavior is not acceptable in our civilization."[17] The quest by these "magnificent two" to save Los Angeles is also a quest to save themselves from stultifying lives. Del and Jen see their vigilante action as personal empowerment, their stepping free from the confining nets of postmodern society, characterized by Del as "the tyranny of class, of gender, of sexual preference, of unrehabilitated language. If it's not one thing, it's another, for us. We're in trouble every which way we turn. We can't move. We're sealed in. We're locked out" (PD 80).

Del and Jen's breaking out and heading west clearly invokes the cultural myth of regeneration through violence underlying the legends of the frontier and the West. But that myth is invoked only briefly: Del and Jen's dream of vigilante action quickly fades before the stunning beauty of the Western landscape, a beauty that leads them to reconfigure their understanding of themselves and their life in postmodern society. Their act of looking down into Canyon de Chelly, Del says, "redefined the world, made it more wonderful than we thought—it was like seeing sky for the first time" (PD 209). In the face of such beauty, their vigilante action seems absurdly meaningless, downright stupid. They give up their plans, Jen says, because "the world is so gorgeous that we can't stop ourselves from going around and looking at it. . . . The reason is that putting one foot in the Painted Desert is more satisfying, more fulfilling, more rich and human and decent, than all the vengeance in the world. This country is making us into saints, making us feel like saints, and that's worth everything" (226).

Through Del and Jen's reconfigured eyes, even the kitschy tourist traps and funky hotels look wondrously beautiful, a fact pointing to their growing awareness that, as stunning as the Western landscape is, they do not need to be in it to be overwhelmed by the world's beauty. That beauty can be found anywhere; seeing it is not a matter of location but of imaginative vision. Knowing this, they now come to see themselves among the everyday cornball tourists flocking about the West—precisely the people upon whom they had earlier heaped so much scorn. Jen's comments about tourists underscore her and Del's own transformations from road warriors into ordinary folk:

> These people are all lovely and sweet. They've come out of their holes for a little bit. It's a pleasure to be among them, to be one of them, to be like them. Because all they want out of their trips is a little bit of first-order experience, a little bit of contact with the ground, a little reminder of the wonder of things. And that's what they get out here. That's what we're getting, too, because once you're out here, all the easy ways you use to understand the world no longer work, and you're left with a mountain or a sea or a river or a canyon. Suddenly, blowing a hole in Damian Williams's face seems like a small idea. Almost every idea seems small and you can't imagine why we spend our time the way we do. Why we sit in our little houses complaining about people doing things wrong, sit there having our little precious thoughts, clinging to our ideas and opinions, arguing for our "beliefs." (PD 227)

At the end of *Painted Desert* Del and Jen reject the pleas of Durrell Dobson, an e-mail correspondent and fellow vigilante, to continue their violent mission. (Dobson is another of the radical individualists whose presence shadows so much Southern fiction about the West.) Instead they are going to swing back to Biloxi, where they will get married and settle down. They are returning, much like Doris Betts's protagonists, to where they started, renewed and remade by their Western journey. Their regeneration comes not through violence but through imaginative revisioning—a change of view that reconfigures the classic American legend of the West.

In *West of Everything* Jane Tompkins writes that Westerns embody a spirit of hard-nosed seriousness, "the opposite of a recreational spirit" (13). Barthelme's *Painted Desert* suggests, on the other hand, that recreation is indeed serious business, that in a postmodern world of commodification and control, recreation is a means for re-creation. The West for Barthelme is not a place to which one flees to escape culture but a place that one visits to integrate oneself back into culture. Barthelme's West thus embodies something akin to Wallace Stegner's geography of hope and possibility; viewing the world's beauty renews one's imaginative vision and sense of wonder. In that renewal, the geography of the West becomes the geography of the mind; the anywhere of postmodern society becomes somewhere, a place to come home to, a place in which to live and thrive with friends and family.

Barbara Kingsolver's celebration of community not only extends that of other Southern writers looking West but also thickens it by reading race and racial identity back into the equation. Matters of racial identity that have always underpinned Southern literature are now played out in a new location with a new cast of characters. In her three Western novels—*The Bean Trees* (1988), *Animal Dreams* (1990), and *Pigs in Heaven* (1993)—Kingsolver revises the American dream of individual freedom into the dream of putting down roots, building families, and establishing communities. Reviewing *The Bean Trees*, Jack Butler writes that Kingsolver's work is "the Southern novel taken west."[18] In many ways this is an apt description of all three of Kingsolver's Western novels, particularly in their celebration of family and community. How fitting that in *The Bean Trees* the image Taylor Greer discovers for the community she helps build in Arizona is the wisteria, that hardy Southern vine. She reads to her adopted daughter, Turtle, about the rhizobia bacteria that nurture the wisteria's roots:

> "There's a whole invisible system for helping out the plant that you'd never guess was there. . . . It's just the same as with people. The way Edna has Virgie, and Virgie has Edna, and Sandi has Kid Central Station, and everybody has Mattie. And on and on."
>
> The wisteria vines on their own would just barely get by, is how I explained it to Turtle, but put them together with rhizobia and they make miracles.[19]

The miracles of human community are exactly the subject matter of Kingsolver's novels.

In *The Bean Trees* and *Pigs in Heaven*—novels that follow the exploits of Taylor and Turtle—Kingsolver suggests that the American experience of moving west has less to do with the dream of starting anew in a world of endless possibilities than it does with being a refugee, with being displaced. This is what Taylor discovers in her flight from Kentucky to Tucson. She has fled west to get away from the confines of her hometown, particularly the fate of early pregnancy and marriage. Her plan, if you can call it that, is merely to drive until the car stops; wherever that happens, she will start a new life with her new name (on the trip out she has changed her name from Missy to Taylor). Taylor gets as far as Tucson, where she attempts to settle in, along with Turtle—the baby she now has in tow, an abused child whom someone inexplicably handed to Taylor during her drive through an Indian reservation in Oklahoma. So much for Taylor's escaping motherhood.

Despite her enthusiasm for being far from her old Kentucky home, Taylor is dogged, almost from the moment she sets out, by a sense of displacement and alienation. She notes immediately upon crossing into Arizona that it seems like a foreign country; she feels she should be wearing a T-shirt she sees on someone else that says "Visitor from Another Planet." Eventually, however, Taylor comes to see that in Arizona she is less like a space alien than like an illegal alien from Latin America. She moves toward this identification in part when she has to deal with Turtle's adoption status, but even more when she befriends Mattie, who helps illegal aliens get settled, and two refugees whom Mattie is helping, Estavan and Esperanza.

It is particularly through her conversations with Estavan that Taylor grows in her insights about the relationship between displacement and America. In their talks she learns about oppression in Guatemala and the choice that he and Esperanza have made in fleeing to America: they chose not to pursue their kidnapped daughter in order to protect the identities of those in a teachers' union who were marked for death. Stunned by the story and knowing that she has never lived in any such place as Guatemala, Taylor nonetheless begins to reconceive her status in light of Estavan and Esperanza's and to question American foreign policy toward Central America and its refugees. She says to Estavan:

> You think you're the foreigner here, and I'm the American, and I just look the other way while the President or somebody sends down this and that, shiploads of telephones to torture people with. But nobody asked my permission, okay? Sometimes I feel like I'm

a foreigner too. I come from a place that's so different from here you would think you'd stepped right off of the map into some other country where they use dirt for decoration and the national pastime is having babies. People don't look the same, talk the same, nothing. Half the time I have no idea what's going on around me here. (BT 135)

Later she thinks that Estavan, who knows by heart the poem on the Statue of Liberty (which begins "Give me your tired, your poor"), must have thought it "was the biggest joke ever to be carved in giant letters on stone" (224).

At the end of *The Bean Trees* the once-footloose Taylor realizes, through helping Estavan and Esperanza find a new home and being helped in turn, the significance of having a place, of being part of a community, of having a network of friends and family for nurture and support. It is at this point that Taylor tells Turtle about the wisteria, and it is here that Turtle sings a new version of her vegetable soup song, now mixing in along with the names of vegetables the names of all of her and Taylor's friends—a child's version of the American melting pot. It is America as melting pot, as a nation of displaced people who have come together to forge a communal identity—rather than America as frontier society, a nation of people forever on the move—that Kingsolver celebrates. For her, regeneration comes not through violence but through reintegration—the reintegration into family and community that closes both *The Bean Trees* and *Pigs in Heaven*.

Significantly Kingsolver's vision of community confronts head-on the issues of race and racial identity, matters that have long polarized American society. Most of this confrontation comes in Taylor's attempts to keep Turtle as her own; her struggles foreground issues of racial identity and heritage, particularly with regard to Native Americans. In a complicated denouement to *Pigs in Heaven*, with a Native American lawyer determined to place Turtle back within her tribe, Kingsolver acknowledges both the significance of racial heritage (as manifested in culture) and the insignificance of racial identity (as essentialized in blood). As Taylor and her mother — both of whom have traces of Cherokee blood — move toward entering the Native American community, they discover that for most Native Americans (at least those in Kingsolver's world) blood is less important than commitment and belief for inclusion in the community. When Alice, Taylor's mother, says she does not feel right in registering as a Cherokee even though she passes the blood requirement, her friend Sugar responds: "Well, that's up to you. But it's not like some country club or something. It's just family. It's kindly like joining the church. If you get around to deciding you're a Cherokee, Alice, then that's what you are." [20] A little later, Sugar tells the still-doubting Alice that registering as a Cherokee requires only a drop of blood and that "being Cherokee is more or less a mind-set" (275). It is something close to Sugar's vision of Cherokee family and community that Kingsolver ends up endorsing here and in her other Western novels, a community that downplays racial markers and differences — skin color, bloodlines, and so forth — and instead strives for a healthy combination of cultural cohesiveness and openness.

Kingsolver's richest Western novel, *Animal Dreams*, clearly celebrates this notion of community. As do *The Bean Trees* and *Pigs in Heaven*, *Animal Dreams* follows the efforts of a young woman to ground herself in family and place. Having lived for years as a fancy-free wanderer, Codi Noline returns to her hometown of Grace, Arizona, to reorient her life. She knows that people in Grace see her as a romantic adventurer, but they do not see how lonely and disconnected she has been. "I'd led such an adventurous life, geographically speaking, that people mistook me for an adventurer," she says. "They had no idea. I'd sell my soul and all my traveling shoes to *belong* some place."[21] Her recurring nightmares of blindness express her fear of being placeless; she realizes that "what you lose in blindness is the space around you, the place where you are, and without that you might not exist. You could be nowhere at all" (AD 204).

Codi's reintegration into her home community involves opening herself not only to love and hope — feelings she has spent most of her life spurning because they involve so much psychological risk — but also to her past as it is configured in her memories. Codi is most at ease in the anonymity of amnesia, of living entirely in the present, but she eventually comes to understand that amnesia destroys on both the individual and the cultural level. Through communicating with her sister, who is working in Nicaragua, Codi understands that the United States is a nation gripped by a cultural amnesia. "That's the great American disease, we forget," Codi observes. "We watch the disasters parade by on TV, and every time we say: 'Forget it. This is somebody else's problem'" (AD 316). Without a past, without the burden and irony of history, America is without a conscience — a problem opposite to the one that has historically plagued the South, which is remembering too much, holding on to the past so tightly that, in Robert Penn Warren's words, "Time gets tangled in its own feet."[22]

If Codi recognizes the dangers of cultural amnesia, she has a tougher time understanding how much she has personally lost by her own deliberate forgetting. Codi has been acting weak and uncommitted for so long that she has convinced herself that this is the way she has been all along; she has forgotten large chunks of her past when she acted forthrightly and bravely. Spurred by several personal crises, Codi eventually begins remembering parts of life long forgotten, parts that show her to be a complex person, neither wholly brave nor wholly weak. She comes to understand that "the human mind seems doomed to believe, as simply as a rooster believes, that where we are *now* is the only possibility. But it isn't" (AD 269).

At the end of *Animal Dreams* Codi takes control of her life by taking control of her memories. Looking forward to settling down and building a family with Loyd, her Native American lover, she commits herself to keeping her memories fluid and vital, neither forgotten nor memorialized but continually revised and reinterpreted. It is a characteristically Southern understanding of memory, similar to that of Eudora Welty, whom Kingsolver most resembles in her comic vision. When Codi first returns to her hometown, she characterizes Grace as a "memory minefield" (AD 46) filling her with feelings of helplessness and hopelessness; but now Grace offers her grace — that is, a place, which for Kingsolver means a home and a community.

In confronting her memories, Codi contrasts sharply with her father, a doctor who has stayed in Grace but who has done everything in his power to erase his past, believing that in order to be accepted by the community, he needed to bury the fact that he comes from a disadvantaged family. He has created an entirely new identity and a new past, one as neatly improvised as the air-brushed photographs he touches up to suit his vision of things. What Doc Homer does not recognize is that action speaks louder than blood. That fact is precisely what Codi comes to realize in her reconciliation with her father, a development helped along by her discussion with Loyd about dreams, particularly his comments about the dreams of animals. After explaining to her father that the reason why he has served the town is less important than the fact that he has done it, she explains: "[Loyd] thinks people's dreams are made up of what they do all day. The same way a dog that runs after rabbits will dream of rabbits. It's what you do that makes your soul, not the other way around" (AD 334).

We are back to Kingsolver's American dream of community and integration, a dream of community that, as Meredith Sue Willis points out, "recognizes no foreigners and is flexible enough to make a place for everyone."[23] It is a dream, as we have seen, in which the way that people act and interact together far overshadows matters of racial identity and class origins. Acting as a community, in other words, a group of people become a community, whatever individual differences and issues exist at the same time within that group. "It's what you do that makes your soul, not the other way around," says Codi, in words expressing Kingsolver's call for a remade American nation.

Kingsolver has been taken to task by some critics for what they perceive as her sentimentality; her plots always push things toward optimistic closure in the face of looming social problems. Although I find such criticism a bit harsh, there is indeed a streak of optimism in Kingsolver—and indeed in all of the Southern writers of the contemporary West (even, on some level, in Richard Ford)—that has historically been missing in the twentieth-century Southern literary imagination. Eudora Welty is the great exception, and oddly enough it may be Welty, the writer most identified with the significance of place in fiction, to whom most of these Southern writers in the end return, rediscovering what she calls "the pervading and changing mystery" of human relationships, "the mystery [that] waits for people wherever they go, whatever extreme they run to."[24]

Epilogue

In his essay "Doing Good Work Together," William Kittredge exhorts Americans to embrace a new mythology in order to understand and guide themselves. The Western dream of radical individualism, Kittredge says, destroys both self and community. "We begin to die of pointlessness when we are isolated," Kittredge writes, and he makes a stirring call for a new American dream: "What we need most urgently, both in the West and all over America, is a fresh dream of who we are that will tell us how we should act. . . . We want the story of our society to have a sensible plot. We want it to go somewhere; we want it to mean something. We must define some stories about taking care of what we've got . . . stories about making use of the place without ruining it, stories that tell us to stay humane amid our confusions."[1]

At the risk of sounding grandiose, I want to suggest that Southern writers who are writing about the West are heeding Kittredge's call, giving us new stories to use in configuring our national identity and purpose. The works I have discussed in the previous chapters have interrogated the American myth of the frontier and have drastically revised that myth from a characteristically Southern perspective. Although I am speaking generally here, it seems to me that the Southerners writing Westerns do most of the interrogating, targeting particularly that legend of regeneration through violence that Richard Slotkin argues has plagued America from its origins up through the Vietnam War and beyond. Again speaking generally, the Southern writers of the contemporary West do most of the revising of that frontier mythology, offering in a vision of community an alternative to radical individualism. Theirs is not a community enforcing restraint and confinement—not, that is, Robert Penn Warren's sleepy Southern town—but a community recognizing and nurturing the independence, the wildness, of the human spirit. In their presentations of individual communities founded primarily on human relations, these writers no doubt at times skirt over some tough matters—social and economic injustice, racial violence, and so forth—of the larger Southern and more generally American societies in which these communities are embedded. Nonetheless, in their looking toward a more just and humane way of living, contemporary Southern writers of the West suggest a first step in the remaking of America and its mythologies.

In its basic shape, the vision of community offered by contemporary Southern writers shares much with that held by the writers of the Southern literary renaissance, with both visions negotiating the borders of place and space. But the recent writers, in part because they break more dramatically and fully from the boundaries of the South—geographically, psychologically, and culturally—recognize more thoroughly the value of freedom of movement. That freedom of movement, by analogy, points toward a more pronounced freedom of thought that is less resistant to time and change and more open to cultural diversity and adaptation. Their recognition of place and space is thus more balanced than that of the earlier writers, who almost always favored place over space, even when they invoked both. Contemporary Southern writers know fully well that place and space need one another for each to be fully present, on an individual as well as a cultural level. Their work embodies what the geographer Yi-Fu Tuan tells us: "From the security and stability of place, we are aware of the openness, freedom, and the threat of space, and vice-versa." [2] And also what Eudora Welty knows: "Sense of place gives equilibrium; extended, it is sense of direction too." [3]

When I was putting together my original Lamar Lectures, two Southern novels about fleeing west were published, both of which strongly suggest this enlarged — or extended — sense of place in contemporary Southern fiction: Tim Gautreaux's *The Next Step in the Dance* (1998) and Dorothy Allison's *Cavedweller* (1998). Because the two are very similar in their narrative shape, describing characters departing Southern small towns for Los Angeles and then later returning home to remake themselves and their communities, and because *Cavedweller* is a bit more wide-ranging and complicated, particularly in terms of psychological trauma and growth, I am limiting comments here to Allison's novel.

Cavedweller primarily follows the efforts of Delia Byrd to integrate herself into the family and town she had years before abandoned when she had taken flight to Los Angeles to be a songwriter and singer in a rock and roll band. Now, ten years later and with a new daughter, Cissy, in tow, Delia returns to Cayro, Georgia, hoping to settle down and be reunited with the two daughters, Amanda and Dede, she had left behind. It is no easy task. The first words she hears upon returning come from a cook in a restaurant who recognizes

Delia: "You that bitch ran off and left her babies."[4] If not always using words as harsh as the cook's, most people, including Delia's family, initially treat her coldly and brusquely. Indeed, Delia faces many tumultuous years of struggle in order to gain full acceptance by family and community.

Underpinning *Cavedweller* is the rather simple idea that over time people change. It is precisely this seemingly innocuous fact that people in Cayro find so hard to accept. As we have already seen, traditional Southern life fundamentally resists time and change, both on the level of individuals and on the level of culture, and much of the tension of the novel centers on the discordance between changing individuals and an unchanging culture. Even Clint—Delia's abusive husband whose violence, we eventually discover, drove Delia to leave Cayro for California—mellows into a forgiving and forgivable man. And of course Delia's return to Cayro challenges the town's rigid structures. To the town, Delia's efforts at reintegrating herself first appear as an attempt to erase history and to start anew where she left off, as if nothing has happened. But actually Delia's return is just the opposite, a facing up to history and responsibility, and it is only when the town comes to understand this motive that she will be accepted, as one of the townswomen puts it, "back into the circle" (CD 70).

As hard as some folks try to keep her out of this circle, Delia eventually does gain acceptance, much to the community's benefit, as it turns out. Indeed, Delia represents a valuable regenerative force for the community, a seed crystal for change. As someone who has been free to roam—has been out West—and who returns home to live, Delia represents the reinvigorating force of freedom and change necessary to keep the town from stagnating and collapsing under the pressure of historical change. Rather than being bound by Cayro, she binds herself to it, bringing energy and commitment to a community that sorely needs people like her to keep it going. It is Delia, for instance, who takes over the hair salon, one of the centers of Cayro's life, and keeps it in business after its owner falls ill. Delia, coming back to help remake Cayro, represents the town's future.

Delia's family likewise needs her life-affirming and nurturing power. Her coming home and establishing a supportive family structure opens up a space for her three daughters to grow, freeing Amanda and Dede from the iron grip of their hidebound grandmother and pulling Cissy back from her wildly unstructured life in California. All three daughters face tortuous paths to adulthood; but all three eventually become empowered and make choices that determine how they will live, rather than being told by others how they *will* live. Although all undergo pressing ordeals and challenges, Cissy's is perhaps the most dramatic, giving the novel its title. Early on, she develops a profound love for spelunking, finding herself most alive and aware in dark sanctuaries underground. Down below, "she knew who she was and where she belonged, the worth of her bones and the cadence of her heart. 'Her place,' Dede would call it. My country, Cissy thought" (CD 324). Cissy's caves are her West— her space of freedom where everything social and cultural falls away. There she faces physical and emotional challenges, having to depend on herself for survival. At one point down below, she overcomes a life-or-death ordeal and emerges invigorated and renewed, reborn. Once shy and withdrawn, Cissy now knows, as she says, "I can be anybody" (CD 409).

Cissy no doubt will soon be leaving Cayro, heading west with Rosemary, Delia's African American friend from Los Angeles, and Amanda will also certainly be leaving with Nolan and their child to start a new life elsewhere. Cissy's and Amanda's pending departures, unlike Delia's years before, will not be impulsive flights from their problems but deliberate efforts to build productive and responsible futures. Although the idea is never explicitly stated, it seems clear that Amanda and Cissy will create circles of community wherever they go — circles accepting and thriving upon cultural and sexual difference, circles founded upon elective affinities rather than prescribed identities.

At the end of the novel, Rosemary suggests to Delia that they should write some new songs. Delia agrees, saying, in the novel's final words, "Yes, it's time for some new songs" (CD 434). These words point precisely to what *Cavedweller* finally is: a new song for growing up Southern and American; a new song celebrating communities remade and rejuvenated through cultural diversity, a mixture recalling Kingsolver's communal vision and Turtle's vegetable soup song; a new song reworking and combining both the Western ideal of radical individualism and the Southern ideal of community.

That contemporary Southern authors writing about the West, particularly the contemporary West, in the end revise rather than completely dismantle a characteristically Southern vision of community points to a striking, almost paradoxical, imaginative motion in their work: the decline in postmodern America of a Southern sense of place, enabling Southern writers to move imaginatively outside their homeland, ends up swinging the writers back toward a grounding in that very same Southern sense of place. "I think if I'd stayed in the South," Allen Tate once said, "I might have become anti-Southern, but I became a Southerner again by going East."[5] Contemporary Southern writers, in their journeys west (not east), likewise become more aware of their Southernness, of their grounding in the Southern imaginative landscape. These writers don't become hard-line Southerners such as Tate became but, rather, renewed Southerners, free and unbound Southerners, Southerners remade through their imaginative encounters with the West.

In their vision of community balancing place and space, contemporary Southern writers of the West in a sense merge Southern and Western mythologies, creating a new frontier mythology more humane and just than either the Southern or Western mythology alone. Intriguingly, this blending of imaginative visions seems to be also at work in the Western literary tradition, which appears to have lately been becoming much more Southern in feel and vision. Not too long ago, Wallace Stegner, perhaps the West's greatest writer, wrote that Western literature is characteristically "not about place but about motion, not about fulfillment but about desire. There is always a seeking, generally unsatisfied."[6] In the past few years, however, that situation seems to be changing, with Western writing focusing more on staying put, on transforming space into place by grounding communities in shared histories. In *The Book of Yaak,* Rick Bass writes that "more and more the human stories in the West [are] becoming those not of passing through and drifting on but of settling in and making a stand" (13). It is a new Western vision. It is an old Southern vision. It is both. This wondrous imaginative confluence, reshaping both the Southern and Western literary imaginations, just may be voicing the new legend Americans need: a national myth centered in individuality *and* community, freedom *and* security, space *and* place. I do not want to call this new mythology the vision of the Sunbelt; I want to call it the vision of America, of America renewed and regenerated not through violence but through imaginative wonder — the wonder of nature, the wonder of home, the wonder of wisteria, the wonder of us all, the wonder of "you and me, here."

Notes

Chapter One: Embracing Place

1. Michael L. Johnson, *New Westers: The West in Contemporary American Culture* (Lawrence: University Press of Kansas, 1996).

2. Wallace Stegner, introduction to *Where the Bluebird Sings to the Lemonade Springs: Living and Writing in the West* (New York: Random House, 1992), xv, xix.

3. The four writers whom Kowalewski identifies as Western are Cormac McCarthy, Richard Ford, Barbara Kingsolver, and Rick Bass. See Michael Kowalewski, ed., introduction to *Reading the West: New Essays on the Literature of the American West* (New York: Cambridge University Press, 1996), 4.

4. Kowalewski, *Reading the West*, 7.

5. I am well aware of the revisionist readings being put forth in Southern literary study, particularly those arguing that notions of "Southern" and "Southern literature" are ideologically loaded and exclusionary, primarily the property of an elite, conservative, white male power structure. Whatever the truth in these readings — and no doubt they carry a great deal of merit — I still think we can talk in general terms about certain characteristics of a

"Southern" literary tradition and imagination that cut across a wide swath of race, class, and gender lines. Regionalism, in other words, still counts in America and in the American literary tradition, even if it is clear in the case of the South that there are many Souths, many types of Southerners, many Southern literary traditions.

6. "Introduction: A Statement of Principles," *I'll Take My Stand: The South and the Agrarian Tradition*, by Twelve Southerners (1930; reprint, Baton Rouge: Louisiana State University Press, 1977), xxxvii. All essays from this collection, hereafter ITMS, are documented within the text.

7. Allen Tate, *Jefferson Davis: His Rise and Fall* (New York: Minton, Balch, 1929), 301.

8. Allen Tate, "The Mediterranean," in *Collected Poems, 1919–1976* (New York: Farrar, Straus and Giroux, 1977), 67.

9. John Crowe Ransom, "The Aesthetics of Regionalism," *American Review* 2 (January 1934): 291.

10. Ransom, "The Aesthetics of Regionalism," 293.

11. William Faulkner, *Go Down, Moses* (1942; reprint, New York: Vintage International, 1990), 286.

12. See Donald Worster, "Beyond the Agrarian Myth," in *Under Western Skies: Nature and History in the American West* (New York: Oxford University Press, 1992), 7.

13. Faulkner, *Go Down, Moses*, 337.

14. Caroline Gordon, *Green Centuries* (New York: Farrar, Straus and Giroux, 1941), 468–69.

15. Gertrude Stein, quoted in Stegner, "Living Dry," in *Where the Bluebird Sings*, 72.

16. Eudora Welty, "Place in Fiction," in *The Eye of the Story: Selected Essays and Reviews* (New York: Random House, 1978), 123. (Welty's essay was originally published in the *South Atlantic Quarterly* 40 (1956): 57–72.)

17. Welty, "Place in Fiction," 122.

18. Eudora Welty, *One Writer's Beginnings* (Cambridge: Harvard University Press, 1984), 114.

19. Welty, "Place in Fiction," 133.

20. Carl N. Degler, *Place over Time: The Continuity of Southern Distinctiveness* (Baton Rouge: Louisiana State University Press, 1977).

21. Lucinda Hardwick MacKethan, *The Dream of Arcady: Place and Time in Southern Literature* (Baton Rouge: Louisiana State University Press, 1980), 181.

22. Robert Penn Warren, *All the King's Men* (1946; reprint, New York: Harcourt Brace Jovanovich, 1982), 52–53. All subsequent citations from this work, hereafter AKM, are documented within the text.

23. Katherine Anne Porter, "Old Mortality," in *The Collected Stories of Katherine Anne Porter* (New York: Harcourt, Brace and World, 1965), 219. All subsequent citations from stories in this collection, hereafter CSP, are documented within the text.

24. Miranda appears to achieve such balance only many years later, in her wanderings through Mexico; see Porter's story "The Grave."

25. Eudora Welty, "Shower of Gold," in *The Golden Apples* (New York: Harcourt, Brace and World, 1949), 11. All subsequent citations from stories in this collection, hereafter GA, are documented within the text.

26. Louis D. Rubin Jr., "Art and Artistry in Morgana, Mississippi," in *A Gallery of Southerners* (Baton Rouge: Louisiana State University Press, 1982), 65.

27. Wendell Berry, quoted in Stegner, "The Sense of Place," in *Where the Bluebird Sings*, 199.

28. Welty, "Place in Fiction," 118.

29. For further discussion of the significance of regionalism in contemporary America, see Charles Reagan Wilson, "American Regionalism in a Postmodern World," *Amerikanstudien/American Studies* 42, no. 2 (1997): 145–58.

30. Wayne Franklin and Michael Steiner, eds., "Taking Place: Toward the Regrounding of American Studies," in *Mapping American Culture* (Iowa City: University of Iowa Press, 1992), 8.

31. Richard J. Gray, *Writing the South: Ideas of an American Region*, rev. ed. (Baton Rouge: Louisiana State University Press, 1997), 230.

32. Julius Rowan Raper, "Inventing Modern Southern Fiction: A Post-modern View," *Southern Literary Journal* 22 (spring 1990): 18.

33. See Fred Hobson, *The Southern Writer in the Postmodern World* (Athens: University of Georgia Press, 1991), 92–101.

34. I should add here that African American writers, for all I can tell, have not participated in this turn westward. Although, as Hobson points out, contemporary African American writers appear at home with many of the traditional characteristics of Southern literature — a sense of place, community, and so forth — their work necessarily reorients and repositions these tropes. Certainly, for instance, "knowing your place" carries an entirely different meaning for African Americans; moreover, from the perspective of the African American experience in the South, being "in place" less suggests being settled than being restrained, in terms both of movement and, more generally, of freedom. Being "in place" equates to being "kept in place." Rather than an east-west geocultural axis, African American writers characteristically work along the north-south axis that has always played such a large part in the African American experience, dating back to slavery and then later to the Great Migration. Although two significant Southern black writers now live in the West, Alice Walker and Ernest Gaines (at least for half a year), their most important work remains embedded in the South and in the Southern experience. If anything, African American writers have looked further south — to the Spanish Americas — for inspiration, particularly in their use of magical realism, as seen in the work of Toni Morrison and Randall Kenan.

Chapter Two: Bleeding Westward

1. Jane Tompkins, *West of Everything: The Inner Life of Westerns* (New York: Oxford University Press, 1992), 6, 12. All subsequent citations are documented within the text.

2. Lee Clark Mitchell, *Westerns: Making the Man in Fiction and Film* (Chicago: University of Chicago Press, 1996), 6.

3. Although certainly the Southwestern humorists frequently looked west

to write about the frontier, they did not write what we now designate as "Westerns." Nor did Mark Twain, though certainly he wrote about the West and interrogated the gap between reality and myth in the Western, and American, experience, particularly in *Roughing It*. This work of Twain's looks forward less to the contemporary Southerners who write Westerns than to those who write about the contemporary West, many of whom write, as Twain did, "road books" about lighting out into uncharted space, both geographic and psychological. The novels of Willa Cather, too, venture into much of the imaginative territory explored later by Southern writers of the West. But Cather is an interesting special case. Although she was born in Virginia, she went west so young and is associated so strongly with the pioneer tradition that her late discovery of her own Southern roots represents a reverse trajectory from west to south.

4. See Richard Rodriguez, "True West: Relocating the Horizon of the American Frontier," *Harper's Magazine*, September 1996, 44.

5. Donald Worster, "Beyond the Agrarian Myth," in *Under Western Skies: Nature and History in the West* (New York: Oxford University Press, 1992), 7.

6. For discussion of the anti-Western, see Richard Slotkin, *Gunfighter Nation: The Myth of the Frontier in Twentieth-Century America* (New York: Atheneum, 1992); and Robert Murray Davis, *Playing Cowboys: Low Culture and High Art in the Western* (Norman: University of Oklahoma Press, 1992).

7. See C. Vann Woodward, "The Irony of Southern History," in *The Burden of Southern History*, rev. ed. (Baton Rouge: Louisiana State University Press, 1968), 187–211.

8. Gene M. Gressley, ed., prologue to *Old West / New West* (1994; reprint, Norman: University of Oklahoma Press, 1997), 12.

9. Patricia Nelson Limerick, "The New Significance of the American West," in *A New Significance: Re-envisioning the History of the American West*, edited by Clyde A. Milner II (New York: Oxford University Press, 1996), 64.

10. Richard W. Etulain, *Re-imagining the Modern American West: A Century of Fiction, History, and Art* (Tucson: University of Arizona Press, 1996), 26.

11. Slotkin, *Gunfighter Nation*, 14.

12. Leslie Fiedler, *The Return of the Vanishing American* (New York: Stein and Day, 1968), 24.

13. James Dickey, *Deliverance* (1970; reprint, New York: Delta, 1994), 275–76. All subsequent citations from this work, hereafter D, are documented within the text.

14. Cormac McCarthy, *Blood Meridian, or, the Evening Redness in the West* (New York: Random House, 1985). All subsequent citations from this work, hereafter BM, are documented within the text.

15. Charles McGrath, "Lone Rider," review of *The Crossing*, by Cormac McCarthy, *New Yorker*, 27 June 1994, 180.

16. Although the Judge is not necessarily McCarthy's spokesperson in the novel, his commentary rules over it.

17. Bernard Schopen, "'They Rode On': *Blood Meridian* and the Art of Narrative," *Western American Literature* 30 (summer 1995): 189.

18. Dana Phillips, "History and the Ugly Facts of Cormac McCarthy's *Blood Meridian*," *American Literature* 68 (June 1996): 441, 448.

19. Phillips, "History and the Ugly Facts," 452.

20. At least one critic has suggested that McCarthy is a writer of the nuclear holocaust even in *Blood Meridian*. In a review of the novel, John Lewis Longley Jr. writes that "the landscape of *Blood Meridian* is like the landscape of the moon, or like the surface of the earth will be after a prolonged nuclear winter when everything is dead." See Longley, "The Nuclear Winter of Cormac McCarthy," *Virginia Quarterly Review* 62 (autumn 1986): 746–50.

21. Cormac McCarthy, *All the Pretty Horses* (New York: Random House, 1992), 12. All subsequent citations from this work, hereafter APH, are documented within the text.

22. Cormac McCarthy, *The Crossing* (New York: Random House, 1995), 341. All subsequent citations from this work, hereafter C, are documented within the text.

23. Ferenc Morton Szasz, *The Day the Sun Rose Twice: The Story of the*

Trinity Site Nuclear Explosion, July 16, 1945 (Albuquerque: University of New Mexico Press, 1984).

24. As Tom Lynch pointed out recently in an Internet discussion group on Western literature, *Cities of the Plain* is almost certainly set in the Tularosa Basin, in the area taken over by the military for McGregor Range, a million-acre tract used for missile tests in the early 1950s. A historian of the region, C. L. Sonnichsen, described the massive changes in the region wrought by the military during and after World War II in his *Tularosa: Last of the Frontier West* (New York: Devin-Adair, 1960), 273–92. Sonnichsen's conclusion was that the Tularosa Basin, once the heartland of the frontier West and the land "where the Old West made a last stand" (281), had become the heartland of the military-industrial complex and its testing grounds. For Sonnichsen, the Tularosa Basin (today, the site of the White Sands Missile Range) lay in this remade West at the edge of a new frontier, "the frontier that borders the unknown land beyond the stars" (292). This formulation, looking forward to the rhetoric of *Star Trek*, stands in sharp contrast to McCarthy's much less romantic vision.

25. See Walker Percy, "The Loss of the Creature," in *The Message in the Bottle: How Queer Man Is, How Queer Language Is, and What One Has to Do with the Other* (New York: Farrar, Straus and Giroux, 1975), 46–63.

26. Madison Smartt Bell, "Zero db," in *Zero db and Other Stories* (New York: Ticknor and Fields, 1987), 155. All subsequent citations from stories in this collection, hereafter ZDB, are documented within the text.

27. In his quest for spiritual fulfillment, Bell's lieutenant closely resembles Faulkner's Ike McCaslin in *Go Down, Moses*: both men seek to establish a way of life based on Native American knowledge, and both end up rejecting the materialistic demands and responsibilities of the modern world for a fundamentally spiritual relationship with the natural world. The lieutenant might be understood as Ike gone west.

28. Johnson, *New Westers*, 24.

29. The expression "today is a good day to die" has proven particularly resonant in the fiction of contemporary white reinterpreters of the West, par-

ticularly for those writers who use their own readings of Native American culture to interrogate Western expansionism. For example, in Thomas Berger's *Little Big Man* (New York: Delacorte Press/Seymour Lawrence, 1964), Jack Crabb explains the meaning of the expression, highlighting the difference between Native American and Anglo cultures: "It ain't the hollow speech it would be among whites. Nor is it suicidal, like somebody who takes the attitude that life has gone stale for him, so he's going to throw it over. What it means is you will fight until you're all used up. Far from being sour, life is so sweet you will live it to the hilt and be consumed by it" (92).

30. Ruth D. Weston, *Barry Hannah: Postmodern Romantic* (Baton Rouge: Louisiana State University Press, 1998), 23.

31. Barry Hannah, *Never Die* (Boston: Houghton Mifflin/Seymour Lawrence, 1991), 119. All subsequent citations from this work, hereafter ND, are documented within the text.

32. Clyde Edgerton, *Redeye: A Western* (Chapel Hill, N.C.: Algonquin Books, 1995), 16–17. All subsequent citations from this work, hereafter R, are documented within the text.

Chapter Three: Regeneration through Community

1. See Stegner, "Thoughts in a Dry Land," in *Where the Bluebird Sings*, 50.

2. Doris Betts, *Heading West* (New York: Simon and Schuster, 1981), 145. All subsequent citations from this work, hereafter HW, are documented within the text.

3. Doris Betts, *The Sharp Teeth of Love* (New York: Simon and Schuster, 1997), 97. All subsequent citations from this work, hereafter STL, are documented within the text.

4. Chris Offutt, *The Same River Twice: A Memoir* (1993; reprint, New York: Penguin, 1994), 44, 121. All subsequent citations from this work, hereafter SRT, are documented within the text.

5. Chris Offutt, *The Good Brother* (New York: Simon and Schuster, 1997),

146–47. All subsequent citations from this work, hereafter GB, are documented within the text.

6. If the Ku Klux Klan represents the extremes of Southern traditionalism, the Bills represent the extremes of Western individualism. The similarities between the two groups are obvious.

7. Rick Bass, "River People," in *Wild to the Heart* (New York: W. W. Norton, 1987), 143. All subsequent citations from essays in this collection, hereafter WH, are documented within the text.

8. Rick Bass, *Winter: Notes from Montana* (Boston: Houghton Mifflin/ Seymour Lawrence, 1991), 7. All subsequent citations from this work, hereafter W, are documented within the text.

9. Rick Bass, *The Book of Yaak* (Boston: Houghton Mifflin, 1996), 2. All subsequent citations from this work, hereafter BY, are documented within the text.

10. Rick Bass, "The Wait," in *In the Loyal Mountains* (Boston: Houghton Mifflin, 1995), 114. All subsequent citations from stories in this collection, hereafter ILM, are documented within the text.

11. Rick Bass, "Mississippi," in *The Watch: Stories* (New York: W. W. Norton, 1989), 126. All subsequent citations from stories in this collection, hereafter TW, are documented within the text.

12. Rick Bass, "The Myth of Bears," in *The Sky, the Stars, the Wilderness* (Boston: Houghton Mifflin, 1997), 33. All subsequent citations from stories in this collection, hereafter SSW, are documented within the text.

13. Rick Bass, "Platte River," in *Platte River* (Boston: Houghton Mifflin/ Seymour Lawrence, 1994), 140.

14. Richard Ford, "Great Falls," in *Rock Springs: Stories* (New York: Atlantic Monthly Press, 1987), 29. All subsequent citations from stories in this collection, hereafter RS, are documented within the text.

15. Richard Ford, *The Sportswriter* (New York: Vintage, 1986), 53. All subsequent citations from this work, hereafter SW, are documented within the text.

16. Richard Ford, *Wildlife* (New York: Atlantic Monthly Press, 1990), 176.

17. Frederick Barthelme, *Painted Desert* (New York: Viking, 1995), 37. All subsequent citations from this work, hereafter PD, are documented within the text.

18. Jack Butler, "She Hung the Moon and Plugged in All the Stars," review of *The Bean Trees*, by Barbara Kingsolver, *New York Times Book Review*, 10 April 1988, 15.

19. Barbara Kingsolver, *The Bean Trees* (New York: Harper and Row, 1988), 228. All subsequent citations from this work, hereafter BT, are documented within the text.

20. Barbara Kingsolver, *Pigs in Heaven* (New York: HarperCollins, 1993), 271. All subsequent citations are documented within the text.

21. Barbara Kingsolver, *Animal Dreams* (New York: HarperCollins, 1990), 30. All subsequent citations from this work, hereafter AD, are documented within the text.

22. Robert Penn Warren, *All the King's Men* (1946; reprint, New York: Harcourt Brace Jovanovich, 1982), 52.

23. Meredith Sue Willis, "Barbara Kingsolver, Moving On," *Appalachian Journal* 22 (fall 1994): 86.

24. Eudora Welty, "Writing and Analyzing a Story," in *The Eye of the Story: Selected Essays and Reviews* (New York: Random House, 1978), 114.

Epilogue

1. William Kittredge, "Doing Good Work Together," in *The True Subject: Writers on Life and Craft*, edited by Kurt Brown (St. Paul, Minn.: Graywolf Press, 1993), 17. Richard Slotkin, too, makes a call for a new national mythology, writing in the conclusion to *Gunfighter Nation* that "we need a myth that will help us acknowledge that our history is not simply a fable of sanctified and sanctifying progress, but that our national experience, and the space we inhabit, has been constructed out of what 'we' have won and of what 'we' have lost by our manner of 'winning the West'" (658).

2. Yi-Fu Tuan, "Place and Culture: Analeptic for Individuality and

the World's Indifference," in *Mapping American Culture*, edited by Wayne Franklin and Michael Steiner (Iowa City: University of Iowa Press, 1992), 48–49.

3. Welty, "Place in Fiction," 128–29.

4. Dorothy Allison, *Cavedweller* (New York: E. P. Dutton, 1998), 39. All subsequent citations from this work, hereafter CD, are documented within the text.

5. Allen Tate, "An Interview with Allen Tate," interview by Irv Broughton, *Western Humanities Review* 32 (1978): 329.

6. Wallace Stegner, "Coming of Age: The End of the Beginning," in *Where the Bluebird Sings*, 138.

Index

Nashville Agrarians. *See* Agrarians
Native Americans, 9–12, 31, 33, 37, 38, 45, 53, 54, 102
Natural world, 28, 38, 44, 45, 48, 50, 54, 80, 82, 85, 96, 97
New Western Historians, 31–32
North, 51; colonizing the South and West, 89; prejudice against the South, 14
Nuclear age: in McCarthy, 48, 120 (n. 20), 121 (n. 24)

Offutt, Chris, 94; and Christopher Columbus, 75, 76; and Daniel Boone, 74, 76; *The Good Brother,* 66, 77–80; *The Same River Twice,* 74–77, 85

Percy, Walker, 25, 51
Phillips, Dana, 43–44
Place: in Southern fiction, 3, 5, 14, 15, 20, 24, 25, 27, 29, 42, 65, 109, 112
Porter, Katherine Anne, 18–20, 23; "Old Mortality," 18; "Pale Horse, Pale Rider," 19
Pynchon, Thomas, 26

Racial identity, 33, 98, 100–103
Ransom, John Crowe, 8, 11, 23, 24; "The Aesthetics of Regionalism," 9–10; "Reconstructed But Unregenerate," 6
Raper, Julius Rowan, 27
Regional identity, 25
Regionalism, 8, 9, 10, 11, 116 (n. 5)
Religion: and Bell, 52, 56; and Betts, 73; and McCarthy, 43–44, 50
Rodriguez, Richard, 30
Rubin, Louis D., Jr., 23

Schaefer, Jack, *Shane,* 34
Schopen, Bernard, 42

Slotkin, Richard, 33, 34, 54, 108, 124 (n. 1)
Sonnichsen, C. L., 121 (n. 24)
South, 51, 71; and its history, 10, 15, 31, 44, 77, 82; and its mythology, 5, 17, 20, 29, 57
Southern literature, 2, 26, 27, 66, 105; and African American writers, 27, 118 (n. 34); and the literary renaissance, 4, 14, 30, 34, 108
Southwestern humor, 118–19 (n. 3)
Stegner, Wallace, 2, 4, 40, 66, 98, 113
Stein, Gertrude, 14
Steiner, Michael, 26
Szasz, Ferenc Morton, 120–21 (n. 23)

Tate, Allen, 23, 112; *Jefferson Davis,* 7; "The Mediterranean," 7–8, 75; "Remarks on the Southern Religion," 6–7
Thoreau, Henry David, 4
Tompkins, Jane, *West of Everything,* 28, 98
Traditional lifeways, 5, 10, 12, 24, 26, 49
Tuan, Yi-Fu, 109
Turner, Frederick Jackson, 11
Twain, Mark (Samuel L. Clemens), 119 (n. 3)

Walker, Alice, 118 (n. 34)
Wark, McKenzie, 26
Warren, Robert Penn, 23, 57, 108; *All the King's Men,* 16–18, 20, 103
Welty, Eudora, 24, 25, 104, 105, 109; *The Golden Apples,* 20–22; "Lily Daw and the Three Ladies," 20; *The Optimist's Daughter,* 20, 21, 23; *One Writer's Beginnings,* 15; "Place in Fiction," 14, 15

West, 8, 11, 39, 40, 71, 75, 79; and
   the destruction of the West, 46–
   49; and its mythology, 1, 2, 16, 17,
   18, 20, 28, 31, 32, 38, 42, 55, 56, 61,
   62, 64, 65, 66, 70, 73, 79, 81, 83,
   88, 96, 98, 107, 108; and the
   Western spirit of expansionism, 7,
   12, 21, 31, 37, 38, 54, 62, 91
Westerns, 4; and anti-Westerns, 33;
   escapism in, 28, 29; written by

Southerners, 3, 29, 31, 32, 33, 34,
   64, 65, 66, 80, 98, 105, 108, 112
Weston, Ruth, 57
Wilderness, 34, 35, 38, 39, 80, 81, 83,
   84
Willis, Meredith Sue, 105
Wilson, Charles Reagan, 117 (n. 29)
Woodward, C. Vann, 31
World War II, 46, 47
Worster, Donald, 11, 30